PRAISE FOR EDWARD HODGE

An ambitious, meticulously researched tour of the idea of crime—from blood feuds to cybercrime—that makes history feel urgent and alive today. It's a rare read that combines sweeping scope with human detail.

> DR. ELENA R. KLINE, PROFESSOR OF HISTORY AND CRIMINOLOGY

An exceptional blend of narrative storytelling and rigorous analysis that traces the evolution of trial by jury, policing, and forensics. It illuminates today's debates on mass incarceration and digital surveillance with clarity and perspective.

> PROF. MARCUS WEI, SENIOR FELLOW, CENTER FOR GOVERNANCE AND JUSTICE

An eye-opening synthesis that links notorious cases with overlooked reforms to reveal that our ideas about justice are not fixed. It equips readers to reimagine the future of crime and punishment.

> DR. SOFIA CHEN, SENIOR FELLOW, INSTITUTE FOR LEGAL SYSTEMS AND SOCIAL CHANGE

THE ENTIRE HISTORY OF CRIME AND PUNISHMENT

THE ENTIRE HISTORY OF CRIME AND PUNISHMENT

WHY OUR HISTORY OF CRIME AND PUNISHMENT MATTERS FOR REIMAGINING JUSTICE

THE FASCINATING HISTORY SERIES

EDWARD HODGE

BOOK BOUND STUDIOS

Copyright © 2025 by Edward Hodge

All rights reserved.

No part of this publication may be reproduced, distributed, or transmitted in any form or by any means, including photocopying, recording, or other electronic or mechanical methods, without the prior written permission of the publisher, except in the case of brief quotations embodied in critical reviews and certain other noncommercial uses permitted by copyright law.

Disclaimer: The information provided in this book is for educational and entertainment purposes only. The author and publisher make no representation or warranties with respect to the accuracy, applicability, fitness, or completeness of the contents of this book. The information contained in this book is strictly for educational purposes. Therefore, if you wish to apply ideas contained in this book, you are taking full responsibility for your actions.

The author and publisher disclaim any warranties (express or implied), merchantability, or fitness for any particular purpose. The author and publisher shall in no event be held liable to any party for any direct, indirect, punitive, special, incidental, or other consequential damages arising directly or indirectly from any use of this material, which is provided "as is," and without warranties.

First Edition

To my family, who kept faith when the questions grew heavy, and to every reader who seeks truth in history—may this book help us imagine a more just world.

If you want a picture of the future, imagine a boot stamping on a human face—forever.

GEORGE ORWELL, NINETEEN EIGHTY-FOUR

CONTENTS

Why We Punish: An Introduction to Crime, Justice, and Power — xv

1. **BLOOD, HONOR, AND GODS: CRIME AND PUNISHMENT IN THE ANCIENT WORLD** — 1
   Eye for an Eye: The First Written Penal Code — 1
   Ma'at and The Egyptian Notion of Justice — 4
   From Blood to Courts: Greek Legal Experiments — 6
   Rome's Harsh Order: Law, Punishment, Citizenship — 8
   Sacred Wrongs and Sacred Ordeals — 10
   Daily Life Under Early Law: Theft, Debt, and Domestic Disputes — 12

2. **SINS, HERESIES, AND KINGS: MEDIEVAL JUSTICE AND THE RISE OF STATE POWER** — 15
   Trials by Fire and Water — 15
   The Right to Punish: Lords, Kings, and Courts — 18
   Clergy as Judges: The Mortal Sin Jurisdiction — 20
   Sharia, Qisas, and Forgiveness — 22
   Heretics and Witches: The Inquisition and the Criminalization of Belief — 24
   Shame, Spectacle, and Community: Pillories, Banishment, and Fines — 26

3. **TORTURE, SPECTACLE, AND THE BIRTH OF THE MODERN STATE** — 29
   The Public Scaffold — 29
   The Queen of Proofs — 32
   Witchcraft and Panic — 34

Monopoly on Violence	36
Edges of Empire	38
Voices of Doubt	40

4. ENLIGHTENMENT ON TRIAL: FROM CRUELTY TO "RATIONAL" PUNISHMENT — 43
- Beccaria and the Revolt Against Torture — 43
- From Secret Files to Open Courts: Transparency and the Rule of Law — 46
- Codifying Justice: The Napoleonic Code and Modern Legal Systems — 48
- Juries and Lay Participation: Putting Ordinary People in Judgment — 50
- Policing the Poor: Vagrancy, Morals, and Social Order — 52
- Revolutions and Rights: Crime, Treason, and the People — 53

5. PRISONS, PENITENCE, AND THE BIRTH OF THE CARCERAL AGE — 57
- From Dungeons to Houses of Correction — 57
- The Penitentiary Ideal — 59
- Work as Discipline — 61
- Women and Children Behind Bars — 63
- Science Meets Punishment — 64
- Resistance and Reform — 66

6. CITIES, COPS, AND COURTS: THE MAKING OF THE MODERN CRIMINAL JUSTICE SYSTEM — 69
- From Night Watch to Police Force: London, Paris, and Beyond — 69
- Crime in the Industrial City: Crowds, Gangs, and New Anxieties — 72
- Detectives and the Birth of Criminal Investigation — 74
- Professionalizing Justice: Lawyers, Judges, and Legal Training — 76

Colonial Policing: Empire, Race, and
Control at a Distance 78
Crime Stories and Public Opinion:
Newspapers, Penny Dreadfuls, and Panics 79

7. SCIENCE IN THE DOCK: FORENSICS,
PSYCHOLOGY, AND THE CRIMINAL
MIND 83
Tracing Identities: Passports and Prints 83
The Lab as Evidence Factory 86
To the Edge of Reason: Why Insanity
Matters 88
Mind over Matter: Measuring Minds and
Moral Worth 90
The Lab's Dark Side and the Promise of
Truth 92
Profiling the Unknown: Crime, Clues, and
the Art of Prediction 94

8. WAR, REVOLUTION, AND
DICTATORSHIP: CRIME AND
PUNISHMENT IN EXTREMES 97
Total War and Emergency Powers: When
Security Trumps Rights 97
Political Crimes and Show Trials: Justice as
Spectacle in Dictatorships 100
Camps and Gulags: Mass Incarceration as
State Policy 102
Genocide and Crimes Against Humanity:
Nuremberg and Beyond 105
Spies, Subversives, and Secret Police:
Surveillance Under Authoritarian Rule 107
Transitional Justice: Truth Commissions,
Amnesty, and Retribution 109

9. RIGHTS, REFORMS, AND REVOLTS: THE
LATE-20TH-CENTURY CRIMINAL
JUSTICE TURN 111
New Codes, New Nations 111
Rights in the Street 114

Health, Fear, and Punishment: The War on Drugs	116
Rising Voices, Shifting Fates: Victims, Voices, and Tough on Crime	118
The Era of Fear: Three Strikes and the Minimums	120
The Prison Boom: Mass Incarceration and Its Consequences	122

10. CYBERCRIME, SURVEILLANCE, AND THE ALGORITHMIC FUTURE OF PUNISHMENT — 125

Hackers, Fraudsters, and Dark Web Markets: New Frontiers of Crime	125
Policing by Numbers: Predictive Analytics and Risk Scores	128
Cameras Everywhere: CCTV, Bodycams, and Facial Recognition	130
Borders, Terrorism, and Global Policing Networks	132
Corporate Crime and Financial Scandals: When the Powerful Break the Rules	134
Digital Trails and Social Credit: Punishment Beyond the Prison	136
Imagining Justice Differently: A Conclusion on Crime, Punishment, and Possibility	139

WHY WE PUNISH: AN INTRODUCTION TO CRIME, JUSTICE, AND POWER

DEFINING CRIME: MORE THAN JUST BREAKING THE LAW

Ask most people what a crime is and you'll get a long list of acts that seem obviously wrong or dangerous. But the word crime is more elastic than a single act. It is a label the law, the state, and the culture decide to apply to conduct. What counts as a crime changes as power shifts, as communities redefine safety, and as new technologies alter what counts as normal behavior. In other words, crime is a moving target, not a fixed roster of bad acts.

This is not just an academic point. It matters because the people who wield legal authority shape the boundaries of social life. They decide which injuries deserve formal sanctions and which harms are left to families, neighbors, or divine justice. They decide who is a criminal and who is a scapegoat, who gets a trial and who gets a verdict by rumor. In many moments of history, the same act—stealing a neighbor's cattle, trespassing on sacred ground, defying a tax or a ban—can be labeled a crime in one era and a tolerated risk in another. The difference isn't only about guilt or intent; it's about who writes the rulebook and who enforces it.

To understand crime this way is to recognize the dual life of law: it is at once a shared shield and a selective weapon. It protects what a society vows to protect, while it also protects the interests of those who write and enforce the rules. The same document that guarantees due process can also be used to criminalize dissent, to widen surveillance, or to imprison a minority for acts that would pass in other communities. Law thus performs a double job: it reflects widely held values and it enforces the power structures that those values often reproduce.

Criminal law sits at the crossroads of morality and governance. Some acts are prohibited because they offend common decency—killing another person, for instance—an instinct that cuts across cultures. Yet many violations arise not from universal moral alarms but from contested political choices. The hunger for resources, the fear of enemies, the desire to maintain order, and the urge to punish perceived weakness all fold into the definitions of crime. The same society that condemns theft may tolerate usury, or may criminalize truth-telling about the powerful. The same nation that celebrates civic virtue may criminalize peaceful protest when it feels its authority threatened.

As we travel through history in this book, we'll notice the way crime definitions expand, contract, or shift focus. The modern world is full of acts that were unimaginable to earlier generations: cyber intrusion, data theft, and the exploitation of information economies. Yet the core tension remains the same: who gets to say what counts, who bears the cost of punishment, and how a society balances the claims of justice with the needs of order.

This chapter sets the compass. We will begin with the big ideas behind crime and punishment—law, morality, justice, power, and social control—and then we'll move outward to the long arc of history that follows. The aim is not merely to catalog acts that led to punishment, but to ask how those acts reveal who a society believes it owes protection, and at what price.

From here, we'll trace the evolution from personal reprisal to public institutions, and we'll ask a simple but enduring question: what, exactly, are societies trying to accomplish when they punish?

FROM BLOOD FEUD TO COURTROOM: THE LONG ARC OF JUSTICE

In the oldest communities, justice often meant vengeance bound to kinship. If a member of your clan suffered a grave injury or a murder, you did not leave it to chance or to a magistrate to decide what justice looked like. You avenged yourself, guided by the memory of the wrong and the power of your connections. The idea of a neutral third party weighing claims and meting out penalties did not yet dominate social life. Vengeance was personal, reciprocal, and highly visible, and it reinforced bonds within the group even as it perpetuated cycles of retaliation.

Over centuries these patterns began to blur. Some societies invented ways to reduce the endless blood debts that crippled households and communities. They created rules about restitution that could be paid to stave off a vendetta. They also began to recognize forms of wrongdoing that demanded collective action beyond the family circle. In places like ancient Mesopotamia and in Rome, rulers and priests began to claim a monopoly on redress, insisting that certain injuries or offenses be resolved by public authority rather than private feud. The shift was gradual, but its message was clear: loyalty to the state, not only to kin, had started to define justice.

The emergence of written codes accelerated this transformation. Hammurabi's law code, one of the earliest and most famous, codified penalties and procedures in ways that allowed distant communities to hear a standardized voice of justice. Yet even these codes still depended on social status. The king's representatives could apply harsher penalties to some offenders than to others, and the line between sacred justice and civil order remained porous. Still, the trend was undeniable: punishment began to migrate away from the household altar toward the public square, toward magistrates, and toward punishments that could be observed, learned from, and repeated without immediate bloodshed.

Across civilizations, other forces joined the shift. Urban life, taxation, and the need to regulate large numbers of people created practical incentives for standardized procedures. In Rome, as in many later societies, legal rules emerged that treated people not merely as kin or neighbors but as citizens with defined rights and duties. Even where violence persisted, courts, judges, and procedures offered a promise that grievances could be resolved more predictably than in the shouts of a crowd.

But the consolidation of state power did not erase the old roots of justice. It redirected them. Public punishment—shAME, spectacle, and ritual—often served as a social technology that taught communities whom to fear, what to respect, and what not to do. The courtroom did not simply replace the battlefield; it reframed it as a contest within a public system, where authority claimed legitimacy through rules, records, and reason.

In our history, the arc from blood feud to courtroom is never a straight line. It is the story of states widening their reach while communities hold fast to memories of harm and the sense that some grievances deserve more than a monetary remedy. As we move forward, we will see how those early steps toward formal justice shaped everything that followed: trials, punishments, institutions, and the ongoing struggle to decide who deserves mercy and who must be held accountable.

PUNISHMENT'S PURPOSES: RETRIBUTION, DETERRENCE, REHABILITATION, AND BEYOND

Punishment has never been a simple instrument. It is a patchwork of aims that sometimes align and sometimes collide. Across time, societies have justified penalties with different purposes, and those purposes have shifted as ideas about human nature, social order, and the state's obligations evolved.

Retribution sits at the core of many early and modern systems: a belief that wrongdoers owe something to the moral order, that certain harms deserve a like response, and that justice demands a proportionate response to a breach. It is not simply about punishment; it is about vindicating a sense of moral balance. But retribution often collides with other goals. If the state's task is to deter future crimes, punishment must serve as a warning to others—the general audience watching. Deterrence can be powerful in crowded cities and industrializing societies where fear of consequences can steer decisions about risk, behavior, and opportunity.

Rehabilitation asks a different question: can punishment repair the person who committed the offense? The modern impulse toward reform sits alongside harsher instincts about containment. The belief that people can change—given education, work, and structure—has driven prison reform, education programs, and treatment for addiction and mental illness. Yet rehabilitation often loses ground when budgets tighten or when the public mood demands swift, visible penalties.

Incapacitation answers the practical need to remove dangerous individuals from the community. Prisons, segregation, and even capital punishment are framed as necessary means to prevent further harm by locking away the offender. The logic is straightforward, but the results are complex: confinement can erode social ties, worsen mental health, and fail to address the root causes of crime.

Restoration adds a fourth track, focusing on repairing harms to victims and communities. Restorative justice schemes bring offenders into direct conversation with those they harmed, as a way to rebuild trust and accountability. This approach challenges the old binaries of crime and punishment by foregrounding relationships and repair rather than isolation and fear.

What complicates these aims is that they often pull in different directions within a single system. A policy meant to deter may increase punishment for the sake of public image, while a program designed to rehabilitate can struggle to meet community safety expectations. Diachronic shifts—from brutal public executions to measured court processes, from solitary confinement to therapy and education—reveal how societies experiment with different combinations of aims, sometimes achieving modest improvements and sometimes trading one set of problems for another.

In this book, we will trace these tensions across epochs and places. We'll ask when a punishment seems justified by its purpose, and when it reveals a deeper register of power, fear, or ideology. The history of punishment is, at heart, a history of competing answers to a single question: what should a just society do when someone breaks its rules?

LAW AS A MIRROR—AND A WEAPON: POWER, INEQUALITY, AND CONTROL

Laws do more than regulate behavior; they reveal who a society believes itself to be and whom it intends to protect. They are mirrors that reflect shared ideals and fears, and they are weapons that shape who has leverage in daily life. In many chapters of history, the legal order has both expressed a common morality and enforced a hierarchy that benefited the powerful. The same pen that writes a charter of rights can also draw exceptions that preserve privilege.

Consider the language of property. The moment a community translates a social bond into a legal title, it creates winners and losers in very concrete terms. Land, resources, and even the bodies of people are subject to legal regimes that determine who may own, who may borrow, and who may be punished. When those regimes are crafted in the interests of a ruling elite, the law can become a blunt instrument to police others and protect wealth. The consequence is not only harsh penalties for the poor or vulnerable but also a legal culture that normalizes surveillance and control over everyday life.

Law's power also shows up in how societies treat dissent. A regime that claims legitimacy by the consent of the governed may still criminalize protest, agitation, and the spread of ideas it dislikes. Importantly, criminalization of dissent is not a distant historical problem; it recurs in different guises—from religious persecution to anti-terror laws to political show trials. The law can be a canvas for moral legitimacy, but it can also be a shield for injustice, a tool for stigmatizing and isolating groups, and a means of extracting labor, obedience, or fear.

The story of policing and punishment often travels with urbanization and empire. As cities grow, bureaucrats build new institutions—courts, police, probation services—intended to manage the crush of populations. The result is a paradox: the same systems that promise order can intensify social control. The poor bear a heavier burden of policing;

the powerful often escape the full weight of the law, maneuvering through loopholes, influence, and delay. In this way, law becomes both a public promise and a private weapon.

We will see, across continents and centuries, how legal forms reproduce and challenge inequality. We will ask who benefits from a given rule, who is harmed by it, and what it would take to align legality with broader notions of justice. The law's power to shape life is vast, and its potential to reform is equally real—if we attend to the history that made it what it is today.

WHAT THIS BOOK COVERS (AND WHAT IT DOESN'T)

This book is a panoramic journey, not a catalog of every crime that ever mattered in every corner of the world. It is organized around core questions, turning points, and patterns that recur across time and space. We focus on moments when a society's ideas about wrongdoing, punishment, and power shift in ways that alter everyday life. The aim is to illuminate the long view—the ways in which systems of policing, courts, punishment, and social norms evolve together—rather than to recount an exhaustive ledger of laws.

Geographically we span ancient empires, flourishing cities, and modern nation-states. We include Europe, the Middle East, Africa, Asia, the Americas, and parts of Oceania, with attention to both well-known episodes and overlooked episodes that reveal broader dynamics. We treat crime and punishment as social technologies—tools societies mobilize to manage threat, shape behavior, and govern daily life. The same tools that produced order also produced exclusion, violence, and unequal access to justice. Our goal is to understand those trade-offs and to ask what future choices might avoid the past's worst excesses.

There are inevitable limits to any sweeping history. Some places lack archival traces, some voices are silenced by time or circumstance, and some dimensions of crime—such as intimate violence or private sanctions—resist easy historical capture. Where sources are thin, we illuminate the contours of what we can know, and we acknowledge the gaps while widening the conversation through comparative perspectives.

This book is not a primer on every legal system, nor is it a defense of any single political program. It is an invitation to see how definitions of crime, methods of punishment, and strategies of power have coevolved. We will meet saints and villains, reformers and enforcers, jurists and citizens, and through their stories we will explore how societies have learned to live with crime—while trying to govern it more justly.

HOW TO READ THIS HISTORY: STORIES, CASES, AND BIG TURNING POINTS

The chapters ahead are built to blend narrative with analysis. You will meet vivid stories—courtroom dramas, prison uprisings, reform campaigns, and quiet reforms—that anchor larger ideas about how crime and punishment operate in human societies. Each chapter places a turning point at its center: a moment when a culture redefined crime, reshaped punishment, or reimagined the role of power in controlling behavior.

Alongside these turning points, you will find carefully chosen case studies that illuminate specific mechanisms—the rise of trial by jury, the birth of professional policing, the introduction of forensic science, or the expansion of digital surveillance. These cases are not isolated events; they are threads in a larger tapestry that shows why systems change, slowly and unevenly, over time.

The prose is designed to be accessible, with a rhythm that mixes brisk, punchy paragraphs and longer, reflective sections. We mix shorter sentences for momentum with longer ones to probe ideas and connect causes to consequences. You will notice recurring themes—the interplay of law, morality, power, and social control; the tension between collective security and individual rights; the way technology expands or restrains enforcement; and the enduring question of whether punishment really makes society safer, fairer, or wiser.

Reading this history is meant to be an active process. Look for patterns across chapters: how ideas about crime migrate across borders when empires rise and fall; how economic change reshapes who gets policed and punished; how social movements reframe what counts as justice. When you finish a chapter, pause to consider what has changed and what has stayed the same, and to ask what future choices might better align security with dignity, power with accountability, and punishment with possibility.

ONE

BLOOD, HONOR, AND GODS: CRIME AND PUNISHMENT IN THE ANCIENT WORLD

EYE FOR AN EYE: THE FIRST WRITTEN PENAL CODE

When we step into the ancient world, the first instincts of punishment feel almost intimate, intimate because they are visible and concrete. In Mesopotamia, around 1750 BCE, a king named Hammurabi had a stele carved with a long catalog of laws. The stone wasn't a rumor; it was a public document, a testament that a ruler's power ought to be legible, predictable, and enforceable. This was not merely vengeance in the old sense; it was state-ordered governance written into stone. The code announced a principle that would echo through centuries: punishment should fit a discernible rule, a standard that everyone could understand. The famous phrase "an eye for an eye" is only one line in a much larger conversation. The law covers debts, contracts, property, marriage, and the everyday friction of ordinary life, not just spectacular crimes. It codified a social order and, crucially, placed the king and his officials at the center of justice, not the family matriarch, the clan, or the local priest alone. It was a turning point: the state as the arbiter of wrong, not only the avenger of kin or the ambassador of the gods.

The Code of Hammurabi is a ledger of practical judgments. Penalties varied by social status—free landowners, peasants, and slaves did not face identical consequences for the same transgression. A surgeon's negligence, a debtor's delay, a merchant's cheating—these offenses all carried specified prices in stone. This was the dawn of written law as a tool of social discipline, a way to limit the brutal arithmetic of kinship a feud often required. The laws are detailed enough to preserve order in commercial life—loans with interest, collateral on property, guarantees of wages—while still delivering punishments that could feel stark: fines, physical penalties, even death, calibrated to the act and the actor.

To modern eyes, the system may feel cold, even transactional. Yet the real innovation lay in creating a shared, public grammar of accountability. Before Hammurabi, retribution was a matter of personal vendetta or divine sanction, handled within the family or the temple. After Hammurabi, the state stands as referee. The code's très public nature—carved on a monument, inscribed in law, meant to guide merchants and judges alike—made punishment a predictable instrument of social control. In practice, what it did was to promote a ordered life in a growing urban economy: formal contracts, reliable property transfer, and standard remedies when misfortune or deceit fractured trust.

The legacy unfolds in surprising ways. The logic and structure of Hammurabi's registry—clear categories of crime, proportional responses, and a written format that can travel beyond the moment of passion—become echoes in later law codes. The idea that wrongdoing harms a societal order, and that those harms require a measured response rather than unbounded vengeance, travels forward. The monarch's justice becomes a framework: it is the state's burden to define wrong, to define the penalties, and to enforce them through a bureaucratic apparatus that can cross villages and horizons. In this sense, Hammurabi's code doesn't merely punish; it teaches a civilization how to live together by rules that everyone can reference, contest, and, perhaps, seek to improve.

And yet this early legal architecture carries a paradox that echoes into present debates. Proportionality in Hammurabi is not just a matter of fairness; it is also a tool of control. The ruler seeks to deter, to stabilize, and to legitimate power. The law's authority rests on a god-ordained cosmology and a kingly vow to administer order. The result is a surprisingly modern mixture: codified rights and penalties, a written system that formalizes grievance resolution, and a framework that invites future reform as societies change their ideas about justice. The first page of the history of crime and punishment thus opens with a dual revelation: the law can be both a shield for ordinary people and a mechanism of state power.

MA'AT AND THE EGYPTIAN NOTION OF JUSTICE

In ancient Egypt, justice is not a distant abstraction but a lived, ongoing effort to keep the cosmos in balance. The very word for truth and order—Ma'at—describes a universe in stability, where harmony among the gods, the king, and the people sustains life along the Nile. Crime, in this sense, is not only a breach of law but a rupture in the ordered fabric that allows rain to fall, grain to grow, and communities to endure. The Egyptian approach to wrongdoing therefore blends moral reckoning with practical governance, and the punishment that follows is framed as a return to balance rather than a spectacle or revenge.

The pharaoh sits at the apex of power, but authority here is inseparable from the divine order. Rulership is a responsibility to maintain Ma'at; to do so, the ruler relies on scribes, judges, priests, and officials who translate cosmic principles into earthly practice. The courts of temple and palace hear cases about marriage, inheritance, contract disputes, and theft, with the aim of restoring equilibrium rather than merely punishing a wrongdoer. In this world, guilt is not simply a matter of what the heart believes; it is validated through ritual and public memory. The heart of a person, weighed after death, is a final test of truth: a heart heavy with crime would be devoured by the devourer Ammit, while the heart that balances with the feather of Ma'at would pass into the afterlife unburdened.

Yet the living discipline of punishment is still practical and visible. Severe penalties are often directed at property crimes, desecration of sacred space, and offenses that threaten the social order or the temple's sanctity. For many Egyptians, justice is inseparable from the idea of cosmic health: forgiveness is possible through ritual purification, restitution to the injured party, and acts that reaffirm communal bonds. The legal world is not a grim stage of fear; it is a daily practice in which the community guards Ma'at by listening, recording, and correcting. The purpose is not only to deter wrongdoing but to sustain the social memory of what the world should be: a place where truth, integrity, and order keep life doable.

This sense of justice shapes everyday life as surely as it shapes temple ritual. When a dispute arises—between husband and wife over property, between neighbors over a boundary, or between a craftsman and a merchant over a contract—the response traces a path that begins with testimony, ends in settlement, and closes with a ritual reaffirmation of balance. The law here is less a ledger of punishments and more a program for maintaining harmony. In the long arc of history, the Egyptian model widens the lens of punishment from retaliation to restoration and order, a move that future generations repeatedly revisit as they wrestle with how to define guilt, how to measure responsibility, and how to rebuild trust after harm.

FROM BLOOD TO COURTS: GREEK LEGAL EXPERIMENTS

The Greek world carries the tension between kin-based vengeance and public justice to the edge of reason. In the archaic era, blood feuds and private vendettas still shape the landscape of wrongdoing. The city-states of Greece begin to test a different arrangement: the community replaces the clan as the primary unit of justice, and the assembly and the courts become the stage upon which disputes are resolved. The transformation is not overnight, but its momentum is undeniable. The early heroes of Greek law, like Draco and then Solon, show a civilization wrestling with what punishment should accomplish when the family's sword is no longer the sole authority, and when citizens—gradually defined—are asked to consider the common good as well as personal grievance.

Draconian laws, named for a king whose name would become a byword for severity, establish a stark approach: the letter of the law is merciless. Offenses are met with penalties that can seem draconian to modern readers: capital punishment for many offenses, and a degree of punishment that makes even minor misdeeds feel dangerous. In a society that valued honor, public memory, and order, such a system serves as a powerful deterrent and a way to teach citizens the seriousness of political life. The fear of punishment reinforces social cohesion and supports the fragile experiment of Athenian democracy. Yet even this harsh static code is only a preface to a more flexible architectural shift: the introduction of citizen assemblies, juries, and a developing sense that law must be enforced through public procedure rather than private retaliation.

Solon's reforms mark a turning point. He reduces the literal cruelty of rules and begins to anchor law in a more rational process. He introduces conceptions of proportionality and fairness, and he creates a framework for legal recourse that allows ordinary people to challenge the powerful. The law becomes a shared instrument of civic life, something that can be debated, revised, and improved. The courtroom, with its judges and jurors, becomes a space where reason and rhetoric can guide decisions. The Greek experiment does not simply replace the sword with the gavel; it redefines who has a voice in deciding guilt or innocence and what counts as a credible witness.

And yet, Greek law still sustains hierarchies. Citizenship remains a central gate through which justice is dispensed.

Free men with political rights stand in a different legal position than slaves, residents of subject cities, or women who have limited public agency. The juries, while representative of the polis, are not a universal mechanism of fairness. Even so, the Greek contribution is profound: the mind turns from retribution toward institutions that cultivate evidence, procedure, and the social virtue of civic life. The stage is being set for a legal culture that will borrow heavily from the past while testing limits—limits that would preoccupy justice in Rome, in Byzantium, and in modern democracies for centuries to come.

ROME'S HARSH ORDER: LAW, PUNISHMENT, CITIZENSHIP

Rome arrives with a thunderous insistence that punishment can be the engine of an expanding state. The earliest Roman lawyers did not simply tell people what to do; they organized the city, the army, and the market around a legal order that could stand behind a vast empire. The Twelve Tables, codified around 450 BCE, are not so much a primitive civic constitution as a practical compendium that makes law accessible in a city where foreigners, slaves, freedmen, and citizens intersect in daily life. The tables cover property, inheritance, contracts, and procedures for dispute resolution. They translate disputes into a common language and a common timetable, a critical step in transforming private quarrels into public matters that law could adjudicate rather than vengeance could settle on the field.

Roman punishment is public, even theatrical. Executions in the forum, public beatings, exile, and a range of corporal penalties reinforce the idea that the body as a site of discipline belongs to the community. The spectacle of punishment serves as a deterrent, a reminder that the state's power is visible and decisive. Yet there is more to Rome than severity; the empire also forges complex distinctions in law that reflect its vast diversity. Citizens enjoy protections and privileges that non-citizens do not. This legal vocabulary—ius civile for citizens, ius gentium for the laws that apply to all people within the empire, and the praetorship's evolving edicts—creates a flexible system that can absorb newcomers and adapt to changing needs.

Roman law is practical and expansive. It invents methods of evidence gathering, formal procedures, and professional roles—jurists who interpret, advocates who argue, and magistrates who administer. The law thus becomes a technology for governing a multi-ethnic realm: it standardizes property rights, regulates contracts for a global economy, and provides a framework within which emperors and communities can live together despite power disparities. Crucifixion may remain the memory of Rome's most dramatic punishments, but the enduring achievement lies in the legal architecture that can knit a sprawling society into a single legal order. In this tradition, punishment serves not only to condemn but to regulate, to harmonize power with the daily labor of living together under law.

SACRED WRONGS AND SACRED ORDEALS

Across many ancient communities, the boundary between crime, sin, and sacrilege is porous. The law turns religious in two complementary ways: first, the gods are often the ultimate witnesses of guilt, and second, religious rituals become the channels through which guilt is cleansed or affirmed. Ordeals—ritual proofs of innocence or guilt—are a familiar instrument. In some societies, a person might undergo a trial by fire, by water, or by contact with a sacred substance, with the belief that divine forces would reveal the true guilty or innocent. The ordeal is not merely punishment; it is a public demonstration of how the cosmos itself judges human conduct. When a verdict comes, the community bears witness to the idea that the gods have a stake in daily life and that ownership of guilt is a shared burden.

Oaths also occupy a central place. A sworn statement binds a person and, by extension, the community that relies on those oaths to maintain order. An oath is more than a personal promise: it is a social contract, a pledge that carries the weight of collective trust. If the oath is broken, the consequences fall not only on the individual but on the social world that trusted him or her. In this sense, justice is inseparable from ritual. Courts and councils may decide an outcome, but the divine sanction—whether invoked through priests, temple sanctions, or sacred texts—strengthens the legitimacy of the verdict.

Crimes that strike at the gods or at sacred spaces—temple robbery, desecration of altars, sacrilege—generate penalties that reflect the seriousness of the offense against the divine order. The penalties are often harsher, the process more ceremonial, and the response more communal. Priests frequently serve as mediators, interpreters of signs, and guardians of ritual memory. The legal imagination here refuses the separation between the sacred and the secular, insisting that acts against the sacred threaten the world's moral weather. Over time, as political authority becomes more centralized, these sacred dimensions fade a little into the background of constitutional law, but the memory of the sacred as the ultimate judge lingers in the structure and rhetoric of punishment across civilizations.

In this way, punishment in the sacred world is a constant reminder that society does not merely punish wrongdoing; it asks the community to participate in the maintenance of a moral cosmos. The line between piety and law remains porous, and that porousness shapes a long arc in which the state gradually learns to domesticate religious coercion into more secular forms of accountability. The result is a history where the divine personifies the moral order, but where human institutions bend to manage that order with ever more sophisticated rules and procedures.

DAILY LIFE UNDER EARLY LAW: THEFT, DEBT, AND DOMESTIC DISPUTES

If we follow crime from the temple to the marketplace, we encounter the ordinary dramas that test early societies most: the theft of goods, the risk of debt, and the friction of family life. The early law codes and ruling practices are not only about spectacular offenses; they are also about the friction of daily life, where the stakes are intimate and the consequences, in the long run, universal.

Theft, for instance, is not merely a breach of property; it is a direct disruption of trust in the everyday economy. A thief endangers the fragile network of exchanges that makes a city function. Punishment must send a clear signal: stolen goods must be returned, and those who break the social contract must make restitution to the victim and, sometimes, to the state. In many urban centers, fines and restitution become the preferred means of redress, because such penalties preserve the possibility of livelihood for the offender while repairing the harmed person's position. The precise balance—how much compensation, who receives it, and how to verify it—becomes a matter of legal procedure, not merely moral rebuke. The law is slowly learning to accommodate commerce and social heterogeneity within a stable, predictable framework.

Debt introduces another persistent pressure point. Loans, advances, and pledges carry with them a risk of default that can cascade into violence or social estrangement. In some ancient economies, debt can translate into a form of bondage or personal servitude, at least temporarily, which introduces a coercive dimension into the law's protective umbrella. The legal response tends to be pragmatic: establish clear terms, set deadlines, regulate interest, and, when necessary, impose safeguards against predatory lending. The aim is to temper hardship with a system that guards the vulnerable while maintaining the debtor's humanity as much as possible within the social order.

Family conflicts—inheritance, marriage, legitimacy, and divorce—are especially revealing. The law codifies who inherits what, how property passes through blood and marriage, and what constitutes rightful guardianship. These cases reveal a society that recognizes the household as a microcosm of the city, a place where trust must be codified into duties and sanctions. Punishments for transgressions within the family range from fines to social penalties, while rules about divorce, adoption, and child custody reflect a broader concern for continuity and social stability.

As these cases accumulate in the record books, a pattern becomes clear. Early law is not a single verdict on moral behavior. It is a set of instruments designed to prevent chaos in a densely connected world: to deter, to restore, to reallocate, and, above all, to keep daily life functioning. The everyday offender might be a petty thief or a bankrupt debtor; the law does not ignore them, but rather seeks to bring them back into the social orbit with a remedy that preserves the community's cohesion. In the end, the daily life of early law is a study in balance: between vengeance and mercy, between debt and dignity, between the rights of individuals and the needs of the many.

TWO
SINS, HERESIES, AND KINGS: MEDIEVAL JUSTICE AND THE RISE OF STATE POWER

TRIALS BY FIRE AND WATER

In the medieval imagination, wrongdoing was not only a breach of law but a challenge to the order of the cosmos. When evidence failed or a case hovered in a fog of rumor, communities often turned to a higher judge: God. Or so the logic went. Ordeals—ritual trials that aimed to reveal guilt through divine sanction—were common across many cultures, from the Carolingian marches to the courts of the Abbasids and beyond. The most famous were the trials by fire and by water, each designed to separate the innocent from the guilty by a miraculous verdict rather than by mortal reasoning. In a fire ordeal, a person might carry a hot iron or traverse a bed of burning coals, with the belief that God's providence would burn away falsehood. If the wounds healed cleanly, or if a martyr's endurance proved steadfast, a blessed outcome would declare the player innocent. In the water ordeal, the accused could be bound and cast into a river or placed afloat in a tub of water. If the person sank, the water was thought to reject the sinner; if they floated or were rescued, they could be deemed guilty or innocent depending on local tradition. Sweat and ash, oath and fear, all mingled in a drama where law and heaven seemed to kiss.

Ordeals were never simple tests of physics. They were social rituals that told communities what they believed about justice: that truth resided in the heavens, not merely in human testimony. To witness an ordeal was to witness belief in a moral economy where God would intervene, where the social order could be reaffirmed through spectacular display, and where the fear of divine punishment served as a powerful deterrent. Oaths and compurgation —where the accused swore innocence with the aid of witnesses who reaffirmed the oath—provided a transitional bridge between direct divine judgment and imperfect human judgment. A person might call upon twelve local peers to attest to their honesty, yet the force of communal memory, rumor, and reputation inevitably colored the outcome. In this way, the boundary between law and religion was porous, and the social square became a courtroom, a confessional, and a theater all at once.

Yet as centuries passed, the aura of certainty around ordeals began to thin. The same societies that once believed God might physically write guilt on a person's skin grew more committed to evidence, record, and reason. The church's insistence that guilt should be proven, not merely confessed, gradually took shape in written procedures and the emergence of more recognizable forms of adjudication. Ordeals did not disappear at once; they receded, tucked away in the memory of earlier practice, but their underlying impulse persisted in new forms. The move away from divine trial toward public, secular accountability did not erase the fear that crime was a rupture of cosmic order; it redirected that fear into structures that could be inspected, audited, and contested in daylight rather than in the fires of the stake.

What began as a belief in God's judgment also reveals a social economy of punishment. Ordeals served to discipline communities as much as guilted individuals. They reinforced boundaries—between sacred and secular, between neighbor and neighbor, between what could be tolerated and what would invite divine wrath. They also exposed the limits of justice when evidence was scarce and passions were high. As a practice, ordeals show how medieval justice stood at a crossroads: a world where the sacred dictated the terms of verification, and where the slow, patient work of building a rational legal order would eventually supplant the blunt force of miraculous certainty. The transformation from ordeal to tribunal marks a broader shift in how societies think about guilt, proof, and the authority that names the line between right and wrong.

THE RIGHT TO PUNISH: LORDS, KINGS, AND COURTS

For much of the Middle Ages, the right to punish rested in large part with local lords who ruled over villages, markets, and fields with the backing of armed retainers. These were not just magistrates in a distant capital; they were the guarantors of order in the day-to-day life of communities. Punishment was embedded in a web of loyalties, obligations, and the fragile peace that kept rival families and neighbors from spilling blood. Each lord curated a jurisdiction, a private yet publicly sanctioned arena in which disputes would be settled, fines levied, and order restored. The act of punishment was inseparable from the act of governance: it demonstrated who held power, who governed through fear, and who could compel obedience.

Across the continent, voices began to coalesce around a new idea: the prerogative of the king to command justice in the broader realm. The move from feudal, local enforcement toward royal jurisdiction did not erase the local; it amplified it. In this period, kings crafted systems designed to interrupt cycles of vengeance, to standardize punishments, and to extend a measure of predictable rule over a sprawling world of lords who often acted as their own petty sovereigns. One powerful engine of this transformation was the creation of a royal judicial order—courts and officials whose job it was to enforce the king's peace and grant a sense of stable law to towns, roads, and border regions.

The shift was gradual and uneven. In many places, memory of the old ways persisted—the custom by which a family could seek retribution under the banner of honor, the private hunt for blood, the village's own tradition of redress. But the crown began to regulate and, crucially, to finance this new system. Charters and writs formalized procedures, while sheriffs, bailiffs, and royal justices began making appearances across the countryside. The famous Assize of Clarendon in England, and analogous reforms elsewhere, began to replace compurgation with a jury system and to reframe the right to punish as a royal, public function rather than a private privilege. The king's investigators started to see crimes as harms to the realm itself, not merely injuries to a noble household, and the punishment as a tool of public order rather than private vengeance.

In this transition lay a fundamental question about power: who defines crime, and who decides the consequences? When the king's officers stood in town squares and roadsides, meting out fines, branding, or corporal punishment, they announced a new political architecture. Punishment ceased to be purely personal retribution and became a signal of state reach. Yet the old world did not vanish overnight. Local customs persisted, and lords still exercised a great deal of discretion in lesser offenses and community disputes. Over time, however, the trajectory pointed toward a centralized justice that could be observed, contested, and learned from across a broader territory. The emergence of royal courts did not erase violence; it redirected it, channeling fear into a system aimed at uniformity, predictability, and the projection of a sovereign's will over a patchwork of communities.

As medieval rulers consolidated power through these evolving courts, the social contract around punishment grew more formal. Punishment began to reveal not only who broke the law but also who maintained the social order. The king's peace implied a public, agreed-upon standard of behavior—an expectation that crimes would be handled in public, with a visible chain of authority that anyone could trace. The result was a more legible map of justice, one in which the line between the criminal and the governed was drawn by the state rather than by private neighbors. It was a long apprenticeship in how power could be organized to prevent chaos, and how the state might hold, weigh, and apply punishment in a way that could be understood, if not always accepted, by all who lived under its rule.

CLERGY AS JUDGES: THE MORTAL SIN JURISDICTION

The medieval world did not separate law from theology as strictly as later times would. The church's power was immense, and ecclesiastical courts operated with a calm confidence that they were administering not merely civil discipline but the salvation of souls. Canon law governed a broad swath of life: marriage, baptism, church property, tithes, and moral conduct often came with legal consequences. These ecclesiastical tribunals could adjudicate matters that secular authorities sometimes found thorny or irreligious: questions of obedience to church discipline, sexual morality, and matters touching the living out of faith. The jurisdiction of clerical courts was, in many places, wide enough to touch daily life in intimate ways. When a community faced a moral crisis—a contested marriage, a charge of blasphemy, or a dispute over church endowments—the church could step in with its own procedures, penalties, and remedies.

The most famous instrument that affected both church and state was canon law, a sophisticated body of rules matured under bishops and scholastics. Punishment could be penance, excommunication, or interdict—forces that could effectively freeze a person out of communion with the broader community. Excommunication severed the individual from the spiritual life of the parish; interdict could pause sacraments for a whole region, pressing rulers and subjects alike to pressure toward compliance with church directives. These penalties operated within a world where spiritual realities were believed to be as tangible as fiscal accounts or criminal records. The aim was not just to deter but to restore the offender to a path of faith and communal belonging.

Ecclesiastical courts sometimes overlapped with secular powers, especially when church property or status involved wealth and influence. A bishop could initiate proceedings that a civil magistrate would respect, and princes might appeal to papal authority to justify or challenge a local verdict. In this shared sovereignty, the line between sacred law and secular administration was fuzzy and contested. The church did not merely condemn the sinner; it purified the community by shaping what counted as a legitimate offense, who could judge it, and what form of remedy would be offered. Yet in practice, the church's moral authority also raised questions about fairness and due process, particularly when inquisitorial methods demanded confession under pressure. The friction between ecclesiastical prerogative and secular necessity foreshadowed later debates about separation of powers, rights of the accused, and the limits of religious tribunals in a changing world.

SHARIA, QISAS, AND FORGIVENESS

In the broader arc of medieval and early modern justice, Islamic legal traditions offered a parallel yet distinct approach to crime and punishment. Sharia, understood by many as the divine law, anchored its rulings in sources such as the Qur'an and the hadith, while fiqh translated those principles into practical legal rules. Justice, in this frame, was a dialogue between divine guidance and human reasoning, shaped by jurists who interpreted revelation to address new social problems. Penalties in this system reflected a delicate balance between community welfare, individual rights, and the demands of God's justice. The spectrum of punishment included hudud offenses with fixed penalties, qisas and diyya, and ta'zir, discretionary penalties left to judges when strict penalties did not fit the case.

Qisas embodies a strikingly victim-centered dimension of justice. The family of a murdered person, or someone harmed by grievous bodily injury, could demand retaliation or the payment of blood money. The idea was to restore balance, not merely to avenge; reparation and reconciliation stood at the center of the process. At the same time, forgiveness and reconciliation remained honored pathways. In many communities, the possibility of pardoning an offender or accepting compensatory payment could close the chapter without demand for further retribution. This emphasis on the victim's rights and the possibility for forgiveness reflects a complex moral economy where state power, religious law, and personal lament intersect.

Discretion, mercy, and proportionality were not theoretical; they played out in courts, markets, and households across the broader Islamic world. The fixed penalties of hudud coexisted with flexible, case-by-case judgments in ta'zir, allowing jurists to adapt law to new technologies, social changes, and regional differences. The state's role as guardian of order coexisted with a robust juristic culture that debated the meaning of harm, justice, and restraint. The result was a legal landscape that could preserve communal boundaries and individual dignity at the same time, even as it recognized that life in a growing, interconnected world would demand continued refinement of the rules that contained us all.

HERETICS AND WITCHES: THE INQUISITION AND THE CRIMINALIZATION OF BELIEF

The medieval and early modern worlds often treated belief as a public act with political consequences. Heresy and witchcraft were not only transgressive ideas; they were risks to social cohesion and the religious monopoly that rulers claimed to guard. The Inquisition, in its various guises—ecclesiastical, royal, or mixed—emerged as an instrument to identify, try, and punish those who challenged the orthodoxies of the community. The logic was explicit: deviation from the official creed could undermine authority, threaten social order, and invite divine judgment upon all. The tools deployed were the instruments of their time—a combination of interrogation, confession, and public stigma. The auto-da-fé, while dramatic and terrifying, was not a mere spectacle. It materialized a moral economy in which belief, belonging, and political allegiance were intertwined.

Across Europe, witch hunts grew out of fear and rumor as much as doctrine. The *Malleus Maleficarum*, published in 1487, became a manual for identifying and prosecuting witches, especially women, who were imagined as rural poisoners, midwives, or troublemakers threatening the social fabric. Trials often hinged on testimony obtained under pressure, tumultuous conjecture about pacts with the devil, and a religious machinery hungry for certainty in uncertain times. The Inquisition did not operate in a vacuum. It overlapped with secular courts, royal authority, and local communities that sought to enforce discipline and protect lineage and property. It also reflected a discomfort with dissent and the fear that single errors of belief could unravel the social contract.

From a historical perspective, the Inquisition reveals both the power and the peril of centralized religious authority. It demonstrates how fear can be weaponized, turning belief into crime and conformity into virtue. Yet it also illuminates how communities argued about the limits of coercion, about who could claim moral authority, and about what counts as legitimate evidence of guilt. The long arc away from these practices did not come from a single reform but from a broad cultural shift toward skepticism about confessions extracted under duress, the gradual expansion of legal protections, and a growing belief that belief should be questioned in open, fair proceedings rather than condemned by decree. The Inquisition thus anchors a crucial tension in the history of punishment: the struggle to regulate belief without erasing the social power of religion, and the reminder that moral order has always carried both sacred duty and political risk.

SHAME, SPECTACLE, AND COMMUNITY: PILLORIES, BANISHMENT, AND FINES

Public punishment in the medieval and early modern city was a spectacle designed to educate the watching crowd. It was a tangible reminder that wrongdoing threatened not just the individual but the entire civic body. The pillory or the stocks stood in the town square, a place where nosebleeds and jeers coexisted with the sharp gaze of neighbors and officials. A wrongdoer could be manipulated into exposing themselves to the crowd, the act itself becoming a public confession that reinforced norms and reminded everyone of the price of stepping outside them. Public shaming carried a heavy moral charge, one that could last long after the punishment ended. It was a social memory that functioned as a deterrent—an attempt to suppress the cunning of future miscreants by turning their misdeeds into a public lesson.

Banishment offered a different kind of social sanction. To exile someone from a town, a valley, or a region was to remove a potential source of trouble while signaling that life outside the community's bounds would be harsh and uncertain. The threat of exile was potent because it severed not only legal ties but everyday ties to kin, work, and kinship networks. Fines—monetary penalties—stood as a more economical and less sensational complement to bodily punishments. They altered the offender's standing within the community, eroded the ability to participate in trade and civic life, and created a subtle but durable form of control that could be sustained without violence. Each of these tools—the pillory, the ban, the fine—speaks to a logic of punishment built around visibility, social bonds, and the fear of collective judgment.

Together, these devices formed a repertoire of social discipline that made communities legible to themselves. They helped maintain a delicate balance: punishment as a deterrent, a reassurance that the social order was enforceable, and a way to co-create a shared sense of normalcy. Yet they also reveal the human cost of shaping behavior through public gaze. The body becomes a map of community values, the town becomes a stage, and punishment becomes a ritual of belonging as much as a mechanism of deterrence. As the medieval world progresses toward more bureaucratic forms of control, the memory of public shame remains a persistent thread in the tapestry of punishment—reminding readers that the relationship between punishment and society is as much about audience as about guilt.

THREE
TORTURE, SPECTACLE, AND THE BIRTH OF THE MODERN STATE

THE PUBLIC SCAFFOLD

Punishment in this era was not a private matter but a public ceremony. The scaffold rose in the center of town squares and markets, a stage where law and spectacle merged. To watch an execution was to witness the state's most explicit promise: that order would be preserved, that transgression would be returned to the social body with interest. The crowd gathered not as voyeurs but as participants in a ritual that bound the living to the memory of the dead and to the legitimacy of authority. The music, the banners, the drumbeats, and the careful choreography told a story about who belonged and who did not. The condemned person moved through a prewritten script—led to the scaffold, offered final prayers, and met the crowd's gaze one last time. The drama was not merely cruel; it was pedagogical, a televised warning before the era of television itself.

Public violence required a setting in which fear could be seen, measured, and understood. The architecture of punishment was as important as the act itself. Raised platforms, prison pits that opened to the public, gallows that could be seen from miles away—each design shaped how spectators interpreted the event. A crowd that's carefully positioned and dispersed—with guards, clergy, and officials placed along predictable routes—receives a clear message: the state has the power to end life, and it will do so in front of witnesses to reinforce communal norms. The spectacle built a social compact, even as it frightened and unsettled the old certainties of kin and clan that once settled scores in private, through blood and vengeance.

This theatre of punishment traveled across regions and centuries, adapting to different climates of fear and discipline. In some cities, crowds heard the news of the condemned's last words before the noose even settled; in others, the officials delayed the moment to allow the crowd to absorb the moral import of the act. The ritual was often punctuated with sermons, proclamations, and ritualized acts of mercy that reinforced noble authority while maintaining a sense of merciful order. The public nature of the punishment served multiple purposes: it educated the populace about the boundaries of acceptable behavior, it deterred potential offenders through visible consequences, and it normalized the idea that violence could be wielded by the state in the name of collective safety.

Yet the theater also revealed tensions at the heart of early modern sovereignty. Observers and critics could point to the contradictions between mercy and severity, between justice and vengeance. The crowd's appetite for spectacle sometimes overwhelmed the legal rationality that claimed to govern the act. As cities grew and bureaucracies extended their reach, the choreography of punishment began to change, gradually giving way to processes that asserted authority without always requiring a crowd's roar. The old square was not abandoned so much as reimagined; the state's power shifted from visible display to procedural sophistication. The theater of the scaffold thus became a hinge in history, signaling a transition from vengeance that flaunted itself to justice that argued with reason, even as it continued to wield coercive power.

The public scaffold was more than a cruel ritual; it was an instrument of social discipline that bound communities to a shared condition—crime, punishment, and the reassurance that power would not abandon them to chaos. In the long arc of the book, this is the moment when the line between spectacle and statecraft first begins to blur in earnest. The scaffold teaches us that punishment was never simply about ending wrongdoing; it was about enacting a social order that could endure the test of time.

And it foreshadows the more intimate forms of coercion that would follow—torture in private rooms, investigations guided by fear, and the gradual shift toward a rationalized system designed to minimize the cruelty of state power while preserving its coercive reach.

THE QUEEN OF PROOFS

Torture did not stand apart from the law; it sat at its very heart, often praised as the *queen of proofs*. In the early modern state, confessions extracted under the pressure of pain were considered sovereign testimony: if a suspect confessed, the crime was deemed proven, and the court could move forward with no further inquiry into truth. The logic was brutal but coherent in its own terms: pain reveals what reason cannot, and the state's job is to uncover the truth even if the path to it runs through the body. Torture was embedded in a legal culture that trusted the result more than the method, or more precisely, trusted the result because the method seemed so effective in the moment. The machinery of torture—rack, cords, the strappado, the boot, the water torture—was not a stray cruelty but an instrument calibrated to press the mind into surrender.

The legal system of the period often framed torture as a last resort after more routine methods failed to coax a confession. In inquisitorial procedures, investigators could push for an admission, arguing that the truth lay

TORTURE, SPECTACLE, AND THE BIRTH OF THE MODE... 33

beneath the skin and within the pain of the afflicted. The burden of proof rested on the accused as much as on the evidence, so a confession could transform into an absolute, unassailable fact. This was not merely about coercion; it was about the very idea of reliable evidence. The court anticipated a certain logic: if the person spoke under duress, the words became the most direct window into the crime. Once extracted, a confession could become the central pillar of a case, leaving little room for pesky details that might complicate the narrative of guilt.

But the realities beneath the rhetoric were troubling. Torture often produced false confessions, evasions, or strategically staged phrases meant to meet the jurist's expectations rather than reveal truth. A suspect might admit to crimes they had not committed to avoid greater pain or to signal loyalty to the interrogator. The danger of error grew with every twist in procedure, and yet the state persisted, insisting that the process itself offered moral and empirical justification. In practice, the torture chamber was a paradox: a place where fear could be harnessed to discipline the body, and where the body's compliance could be misread as moral clarity. Across provinces and kingdoms, judges and clerks justified their methods by appeals to necessity and expedience, while critics warned that the very tools used to reveal truth often concealed something more troubling—arbitrary power masquerading as legal certainty.

The towering confidence in torture's efficacy began to erode, not through a single act of rebellion but through a broader shift in how justice was imagined. Philosophers, jurists, and reformers began to challenge the idea that suffering could be a reliable instrument of discovery. They argued that truth should be sought through impartial procedures that protected the accused as a matter of principle, not merely as a gesture of humanity. The decline of torture was not abrupt; it came as a slow rebalancing of power, a redefinition of what counted as credible evidence, and a growing belief that the legitimacy of the state rests as much on fairness as on force. In this transitional moment, the "queen" began to lose her crown, even as she continued to influence the design of law and punishment for generations to come.

WITCHCRAFT AND PANIC

The Great Witch Hunts illuminate a crucial tension in the birth of the modern state: how fear, religion, and social strain could be weaponized to claim authority. Witchcraft accusations proliferated in periods of upheaval, when markets faltered, crops failed, and communities felt unstable under the pressure of conflict and famine. The apparatus of state power—courts, magistrates, priests, and neighborly networks—could be marshaled to identify a scapegoat who embodied danger to the community's moral order. As accusations spread, the legal process

TORTURE, SPECTACLE, AND THE BIRTH OF THE MODE... 35

became a stage for dramatized belief, and fear became as powerful a form of evidence as any confession won by pain. The state's prerogative to identify danger was reinforced by a narrative in which witches stood at the center of malevolent forces—pagan or religious, ancient or modern—threatening the social fabric.

Witch trials were not merely fanatical outliers; they reflected deeper anxieties about gender, social order, and religious purity. In many communities, women—especially those who were poor, widowed, or intellectually autonomous—carried a disproportionate share of suspicion. The accusation became a social weapon: it could police property, regulate inheritance, and discipline community dissent. Yet the witch hunts also reveal a surprising logic of legal proceedings. Authorities relied on spectral evidence, confessions wrung under duress, and the authority of learned men who could interpret the signs of the devil's influence. These elements created an intoxicating mix of fear and certainty that could be harnessed to suppress rivals, settle feuds, or consolidate political power.

The scale of the hunts varied by region, but the pattern was remarkably consistent: a public campaign that framed social anxiety as a cosmological crisis requiring urgent intervention. The spectacle of trials, interrogations, and executions served as a visible reminder that disorder would not be tolerated. But as the century wore on, the weight of experience and the resurgence of rational inquiry began to chip away at the edifice. Judges who once relied on punitive zeal started demanding more robust, secular grounds for conviction. The decline was gradual and contested, often stunted by lingering superstitions and institutional inertia. Yet the larger arc was clear: the state's authority to decide who was dangerous had to be tempered by the recognition that fear is not a substitute for evidence, and that the social body itself would be healthiest when restraint and reason guided its most coercive powers.

MONOPOLY ON VIOLENCE

The emergence of absolutist polities did more than centralize power; it redefined what a state could claim as its exclusive right. The monopoly on violence—often summarized as the idea that the sovereign alone may wage coercion—was not merely a slogan but a reorganizing principle. Rulers argued that a sovereign's legitimacy depended on the ability to prevent, deter, and punish crime with certainty and efficiency. In practice, this meant the creation of centralized bureaucracies, professional administrators, and standing institutions that could reach into every village and harbor. The old patchwork of private feuds and ad hoc justice gave way to standardized laws, regular courts, and a formal police that could operate across borders as the state's eyes and hands.

The monopolization of force was inseparable from a new rationality of punishment. Instead of public vengeance that anyone with a grievance could exact, punishment became a state-managed process governed by rules, schedules, and predictable penalties. Armies shifted from feudal levies to professional forces; courts standardized procedures, reducing the unpredictability that private vengeance thrived on. Prisons, although evolving slowly, became a core piece of the system, confining offenders for defined periods with the hope of reform or at least the reduction of harm to society. The state's claim to violence also required a narrative: that punishment protected the common good, that it deterred future misdeeds, and that it did so in a way that was ultimately legible to the public understanding of justice. This new order did not end the use of coercion; it reoriented it toward a centralized, bureaucratic mechanism designed to be, in theory at least, more equitable than the old theatre of vengeance.

Crucially, the monopoly on violence enabled a more confident claim that cruelty could be civilized. It justified the expansion of state power in the name of social order while also inviting constant scrutiny from reformers who argued for constraint, proportionality, and constitutional checks. The stage had changed, but the script—punishment as a means of shaping social life—remained: a powerful instrument that could define legitimacy as well as fear. In the long arc of this story, the state's right to punish becomes a question not only of safety but of how a civilization understands itself—as a community capable of restraining its own power, or as a system that must continually negotiate the line between protection and coercion.

EDGES OF EMPIRE

To imagine punishment only within the tidy walls of a capital city is to miss a vast and unruly frontier: the borders where empire met its critics, where bandits and pirates defied the authority of distant rulers, and where the state's right to punish was most severely tested. Bandits roamed the countryside as if the law had grown thin on the margins, while pirates ruled a breaking world of seas and ports, where law was as much a matter of practical force as it was of decrees carved on parchment. In these outer domains, crime was less a private grievance than a political problem: how to maintain order where roads were unsafe, ships vulnerable, and local loyalties volatile.

The state responded by redefining who counted as an enemy and by expanding its reach in ways that often blurred lines between justice and commerce. Pirates, celebrated in ballads and feared in statehouses, inhabited a paradox: they could be criminals in one jurisdiction and emboldened agents of anti-imperial resistance in another, especially when their actions disrupted rival empires' trade routes. The state's solution was not simply punishment but legal reform: codifying what piracy meant, legitimizing some forms of private violence against enemies of the crown, and creating maritime courts that could adjudicate transoceanic crimes far from home shores. This patchwork system—maritime codes alongside land-based penal practices—demonstrated how cruel coercion could be deployed abroad with the same confidence as at home, validating the empire's power by demonstrating its reach.

Banditry and piracy fed an enduring ambivalence about law and order: criminals could be both enemies of the state and tools of the state's expansion. When governors captured or executed a pirate captain, the act carried multiple messages— victory over a rival power, the protection of commerce, and a warning that the sea would be policed in the empire's name. The moral economy of punishment thus extended beyond borders, and the fear of roaming violence reminded communities that security demanded constant vigilance. Yet the outer towns and ports also offered a different picture: a marketplace of negotiated violence, where local elites sometimes concealed complicity or profited from the very disorder they claimed to suppress. The frontier thus became a crucible in which the meanings of crime, punishment, and sovereignty were rewritten for a world that was increasingly interconnected, competitive, and anxious about who controlled the routes that carried goods, people, and ideas.

The era's most dramatic changes did not erase the old ideas of justice; they reframed them. The state's claim to exercise power at the edges of empire required new forms of legitimacy and new technologies of control: faster communications, standardized tariffs, piracy laws, and imperial courts that worked across seas. It also forced a reckoning with the limits of state coercion: if a ruler could extend punishment to distant waters, could punishment also be kept humane and proportionate in more intimate settings? The answers varied by place and by era, but the impulse to regulate crime through a dangerous blend of spectacle, fear, and legal form remained a defining feature of this chapter's century—and a precondition for the modern system that would follow.

VOICES OF DOUBT

In the shadow of spectacle and state power, a handful of voices dared to question the very assumptions that justified cruelty. They did not always win immediate triumphs, but their ideas traveled far enough to stir new sensibilities about justice, evidence, and the purpose of punishment. The most famous of these voices is Cesare Beccaria, whose *On Crimes and Punishments* argued that punishment should be certain, swift, and proportionate, and that the state owed citizens a rational and humane framework for judging guilt. Beccaria challenged the central premise that suffering itself was a reliable teacher. He argued that cruelty corrupts both the body and the social contract, eroding legitimacy and inspiring calculated resistance. His prose was not a manifesto for immediate abolition but a roadmap for reform: limit the use of pain, end hidden arbitrariness, and replace coercive tactics with predictable, evidence-based procedures.

Beccaria stood on a chorus of Enlightenment thinkers who suspected that authority, when left unchecked, would lean toward cruelty as a default setting. Voltaire's incisive sarcasm and Montesquieu's insistence on moderating power joined a broader critique of superstition, religious intolerance, and law's capacity for oppression. The project of reform became a dialogue between reform-minded jurists and a public increasingly willing to debate how crime should be defined and punished. At times, these arguments clashed with the logics of rulers who sought order through fear. Yet even in periods of political stagnation or reaction, the seeds of critique found soil: in newspapers, salons, magistrate offices, and treatises that insisted legality must be intelligible and humane if it was to be legitimate.

Material improvements—prison reforms, clearer procedures, and more transparent trials—began to appear alongside philosophical critiques. Critics drew attention to the human cost of violence, the risk of false confessions, and the social damage wrought by fear and vengeance. They urged the creation of institutions that could provide due process for the accused and protections for the innocent. While reformers faced resistance—often brutal, sometimes incremental—they laid the groundwork for a transformation that would unfold over generations. In the pages that follow, the critique would move from the realm of ideas into the realm of institutions: the sciences of law, the practicality of reform, and the political will to reimagine crime and punishment not as a matter of raw power but as a shared project of justice.

FOUR
ENLIGHTENMENT ON TRIAL: FROM CRUELTY TO "RATIONAL" PUNISHMENT

BECCARIA AND THE REVOLT AGAINST TORTURE

In a candlelit study in a European city, a young professor asks a stubborn question that echoes through centuries: can a state justify cruelty in the name of justice? Cesare Beccaria answered no. His pamphlet On Crimes and Punishments, published in 1764, did not merely argue for milder penalties; it argued for a complete rethinking of punishment as a social instrument. The aim of law, he said, is to prevent crime and to secure the greatest good for the greatest number. Cruelty, he insisted, is not a legitimate tool of policy; it corrupts both the offender and the state that enforces it.

Beccaria's central thesis was startling in its clarity. Laws should be clear, known to all, and applied equally.

Penalties should be proportionate to the crime and applied with a sense of moderation rather than terror. Most radical of all, punishment should be certain rather than extreme: a predictable consequence of wrongdoing, not a ritual of spectacle or a tool to frighten the population into obedience. He rejected torture as an unreliable method for uncovering truth, arguing that pain distorts it. If a confession comes only under the lash, it is no confession at all; it is a manufactured instrument of fear.

The idea that the state's legitimate authority rests on reason, rather than fear, was a cornerstone of Enlightenment thinking. Beccaria's critique extended beyond torture to the broader architecture of criminal law. He urged legislators to write down offenses and penalties, to abolish ambiguous and capricious rules, and to ensure that laws operate on principals accessible to all citizens. The point was not merely to spare offenders from excess but to curb the political temptations that accompany arbitrary punishment: rulers who punish to demonstrate their power rather than to protect the common good.

Beccaria's vision spread with remarkable speed. Philosophers and jurists translated his ideas across borders, seeding reforms in states with very different political cultures. In Prussia, Austria, and Russia, legal reformers borrowed his insistence on proportionality and restraint. The long shadow of Beccaria's argument can be traced in the gradual shifts from spectacular punishment to surveillance, from secret coercion to codified rights, and from fear as a governing principle to law as a constraint on power. Yet the translation from pamphlet to practice was uneven. Courts and rulers often found ways to preserve the prestige of punishment even as they adopted its more humane rhetoric.

The practical influence of Beccaria's argument lay not in immediate abolition but in a systematizing of the idea that punishment should serve public welfare, not private vengeance. It encouraged jurists to demand clearer procedures, more predictable sentences, and less room for the arbitrariness that had flourished under monarchical or inquisitorial regimes. In time, his ideas helped fuel reforms that would give ordinary people certain protections in the face of authority, and they provided a moral vocabulary for challenging cruel traditions that had long framed crime as a private, rather than a public, concern.

Beccaria's revolt against torture did more than quash a cruel instrument of governance. It redefined the logic of law itself. If the state is to be legitimate, it must be able to answer to reason and to the governed, not just to the will of the powerful. The Enlightenment thus began its enduring project: to turn punishment into a rational process governed by law, evidence, and proportional justice rather than by fear and spectacle.

FROM SECRET FILES TO OPEN COURTS: TRANSPARENCY AND THE RULE OF LAW

If Beccaria argued for rational limits on punishment, the next great leap was to insist that justice be visible. The movement from secret to public procedures was not instantaneous; it unfolded across decades and across continents, reshaping the social contract between state power and ordinary citizens. The old order trusted officials to decide guilt behind closed doors, with the public and the accused isolated from meaningful scrutiny. Enlightenment thinkers challenged this secrecy, arguing that the legitimacy of punishment depended on the people seeing the process and judges reasoning in sunlit reasoning rather than in shadowy coercion.

Public trials emerged as a democratic and philosophical problem of the first order. When trials take place in public, arguments must be made in front of witnesses, jurors, and the public, rather than behind a curtain of inquisitorial ritual or imperial discretion. The courtroom becomes a stage where the accused can present a defense, the prosecution must disclose evidence, and the presumption of innocence gains practical meaning through every obstacle course of procedure. The shift also meant that laws themselves needed to be accessible. If citizens are to be judged by reason, they must understand the terms of the law—what constitutes a crime, what penalties follow, and why.

Across Europe and its spheres of influence, judges, lawyers, and reformers pressed for procedures that could be inspected by the public. The move toward adversarial procedures in many jurisdictions accompanied the growth of professional legal cultures—trained prosecutors, defense counsel, and court reporters who could translate complex debates into accessible explanations for lay audiences. The press began to play a more critical role, not as an apologist for state power but as a watchdog that could expose abuses, highlight inconsistencies, and remind the public that justice should answer to reason and evidence rather than to fear or favoritism.

Even as breakthroughs toward openness took root, the work did not end with a single reform. The new transparency demanded accompanying protections: the right to present witnesses, the right to challenge evidence, limitations on arbitrary detention, and the guarantee that trials would be conducted within a framework of due process. The law, once a veil drawn by the powerful, now required a compelling rationale for any deviation from the standard rules. The result was a legal culture in which the public could observe the functioning of law, and where the accountability of judges, prosecutors, and officials was bound to argument, record, and reason.

The broader significance of transparency reached beyond courts. As procedures became public, the habit of accountability spread into legislative debate, administrative rulemaking, and even how societies discuss crime and punishment in the public square. The idea that the state governs by standards that can be checked, debated, and revised—rather than by fear or force—became a durable feature of modern legal systems. The public trial, in its many forms, became the indispensable instrument through which citizens could judge whether law served the common good.

CODIFYING JUSTICE: THE NAPOLEONIC CODE AND MODERN LEGAL SYSTEMS

The early 19th century brought a radical reorganization of law: law should not float in the air as a collection of scattered edicts but be gathered into a coherent, accessible system. The Napoleonic Code, formally introduced in 1804, stood at the center of this transformation. It was a consciously modern project: to discipline the variety of regional laws into a unified framework, to treat citizens as equals before the law, and to routinize the administration of justice under a centralized state. The code did not merely rewrite penalties; it changed the language of law, turning regulations into explicit rules that could be learned, taught, and applied with predictability.

The Code took the Enlightenment's insistence on rational legality and embedded it into everyday life. Crimes and penalties were enumerated, defined, and standardized. The distance between intent and consequence was narrowed by clearer statutes and more formal procedures. Across France and in territories touched by French influence, the Napoleonic Code reshaped the procedures of courts, the organization of police networks, and the training of jurists. In effect, it created a model for modern legal systems that many other nations would imitate or adapt: a single, codified set of laws that could travel across borders through conquest, colonization, or reform.

Yet codification was not a quiet act of emancipation. It also extended the reach and power of the state. Centralization meant that magistrates and prosecutors could wield uniform authority across vast territories. The code sometimes preserved harsh penalties and the sovereign prerogative of punishment in new, carefully rationalized forms. Still, the code's insistence on consistency, clarity, and the rule of law helped undermine the old, improvisational justice of local rulers. It offered a rational framework within which judges could interpret guilt, determine sentences, and appeal to a universal measure of justice rather than personal whim.

In the long arc of history, the Napoleonic Code became a foundational reference point for many civil-law jurisdictions. Its influence spread far beyond the shores of France, shaping European and Latin American legal cultures for generations. It helped to seed the modern idea that law should anticipate human behavior through codified rules, making the system less a theater of punishment and more a mechanism for securing predictable outcomes, even as it also consolidated a centralized state's capacity to enforce those outcomes.

JURIES AND LAY PARTICIPATION: PUTTING ORDINARY PEOPLE IN JUDGMENT

The idea that legal judgments should involve ordinary people as participants rather than only trained officials marked a turning point in the legitimacy of punishment. The jury, as a transitional instrument between autocratic decree and popular sovereignty, offered a compelling answer to the question: who should decide guilt? The concept of a jury of one's peers carried ancient echoes, but its modern imprint grew strongest in the long march of the 18th and 19th centuries. Juries were presented as a safeguard against the arbitrary exercise of state power, a way to ensure that judgments reflected communal norms and common sense rather than the capricious will of rulers or magistrates.

However, the jury was not an unproblematic instrument. Who counted as a peer? Eligibility often hinged on property, class, and citizenship. Debates over inclusion reflected broader questions about democracy, equality, and social advantage. Yet the very struggle to articulate who could sit in judgment revealed an aspirational truth: ordinary people could, under the right conditions, make fair and reasoned judgments. The adoption and adaptation of jury trials varied by country, but a shared conviction underpinned many reforms: public, lay participation could both educate the public about the law and hold the state to account through the spectacle and discipline of communal adjudication.

The jury became more than a legal mechanism; it was a symbol. It signified that law was a shared enterprise, not a private instrument of rulers. The juries' presence helped democratize the trial, enabling a broader public to witness the processes by which crime was defined, guilt established, and penalties assigned. It also sparked crucial debates about the limits of lay judgment—about bias, class dynamics, and the risks of crowdthink infiltrating the courtroom.

As the 19th century progressed, juries helped spur parallel reforms: more open elections, wider literacy, and increased public investment in education and the press. The jury, in short, linked the courtroom to the broader political project of making law legible and controllable by ordinary citizens. It was one of the Enlightenment's most enduring legacies: the belief that ordinary people could participate in the moral life of the community through the slow, careful work of judging each other's conduct.

POLICING THE POOR: VAGRANCY, MORALS, AND SOCIAL ORDER

If Beccaria and the codes set limits on punishment, the next frontier of Enlightenment-era reform was the policing of everyday life—the management of poverty, sexuality, and public behavior. As cities swelled with new workers, markets expanded, and the social fabric strained, authorities sought to shape behavior through law. The result was a new model of social order in which punishment extended beyond the crime itself to the surveillance of habit, poverty, and morality. Vagrancy laws became a central tool. The naked question behind them was not simply "Did you break the law?" but "Who are we allowed to be in public?"

Vagrants—beggars, wanderers, and the unemployed—were quickly defined as a social problem that required correction through disciplined oversight. The response combined public order with moral instruction. Begging, loitering, sleeping in the streets, or consorting near taverns could be treated as offenses, and penalties could include fines, corporal punishment, or compulsory work. The logic was clear: it was prudent to reshape the behavior of the least fortunate before their behavior corrupted respectable society. The line between social policy and punishment blurred, as reformers justified coercion as a humane attempt to rehabilitate rather than simply to punish.

Police reorganized around this moral project. The emergence of professional police forces—most famously in the United Kingdom with the 1829 Metropolitan Police—marked a change in the scale and texture of social control. Officers were placed on the street to prevent crime, but they were also tasked with enforcing the moral codes that defined public life. Public morality campaigns—restrictions on vice, curfews, controls on sexuality, and the policing of public spaces—became standard features of urban life. The effect was twofold: a more orderly city, and a population that began to experience state presence as a continuous, visible reality in their daily routines.

This expansion of police power raised difficult questions that echo to this day. How do societies balance public safety with civil liberties, especially for the most vulnerable? How do we determine what counts as reform versus punishment? The answers varied by place and time, but the impulse remained consistent: to regulate the social body through law, in order to channel disruptive forces—poverty, desire, dissent—into forms that could be managed, contained, and, ideally, redirected toward what authorities framed as the public good.

REVOLUTIONS AND RIGHTS: CRIME, TREASON, AND THE PEOPLE

Revolution has a way of clarifying a society's deepest choices about crime and punishment. When political order is upended, the line between "criminal" and "hero" often seems unsettled. The same moment that produced new social contracts also produced new expectations about due process, rights, and the limits of state power. The aftermath of revolutions—whether in the French, American, or later European contexts—put rights and the rule of law on trial, not merely the criminals themselves.

The French Revolution, with its Declaration of the Rights of Man and of the Citizen, asserted that sovereignty resides in the people and that law should reflect universal principles of liberty, equality, and fraternity. Yet within the revolutionary momentum lurked a paradox: the same upheaval that promised political liberty could unleash coercive devices designed to crush counterrevolutionaries. Revolutionary tribunals and extraordinary measures enabled swift punishments and mass surveillance, while constitutional debates began to demand due process, fair trials, and legal restraint. The tension between defending the republic and defending individual rights became a crucible through which modern criminal justice would be forged.

In the American sphere, the creation of a constitutional order that protected individual rights—free speech, due process, and protection against arbitrary detention—helped reframe punishment as a bounded power. The Bill of Rights, and later due-process jurisprudence, anchored the state's authority in procedures that could be publicly scrutinized and contested. Across Europe, reformers argued that criminal law should reflect the people's consent through institutions that could check executive power. Rights movements—civil rights campaigns, labor struggles, and anti-colonial campaigns—fed into a broader insistence that punishment must adhere to rational standards, not merely to the ruler's will.

The revolutions also redefined what counted as a crime. Treason and sedition, once the most direct means of suppressing political rivals, were slowly reimagined as offenses to be constrained by legal process and public scrutiny. The new lexicon of rights recast the state's power as a public trust. The law became a platform for negotiation about who belongs, who is protected, and how dissent is to be treated. As these ideas dispersed, they shaped not only criminal procedure but the very meaning of citizenship and inclusion within the political community.

Looking forward, this era of upheaval seeded the modern project: to build criminal justice on principles that could endure war, revolution, and reform. It laid the groundwork for the postwar turn toward universal rights, fair trials, and protections against the worst excesses of state power. It also left a persistent challenge: to translate abstract rights into actual protections for the most vulnerable, in a world where political necessity and public fear continue to press in opposite directions.

FIVE
PRISONS, PENITENCE, AND THE BIRTH OF THE CARCERAL AGE

FROM DUNGEONS TO HOUSES OF CORRECTION

In the long arc from brutal dungeons to more orderly houses of correction, confinement began as a response to chaos rather than a plan for reform. Medieval and early modern jails were often grim, sticky places carved from stone where debtors, debtors' wardens, and petty criminals mingled with enemies of the state. It was a system built on visibility and fear: the garrisoned fortresses, the dark cell, the executioner's scaffold. Yet across Europe and the Atlantic world a new idea took shape. Prisons began to separate the merely restless from the truly dangerous, and then to discipline those who were kept behind walls. The shift did not happen overnight, nor did it arrive with one grand theory. It arrived as a series of experiments, each one rewriting the promise of punishment.

In Britain, the term house of correction emerged as urban authorities sought a more respectable, more manageable form of containment for petty offenders. The Bridewell, a word that would become shorthand for a kind of municipal jail turned workhouse, embodied this new logic: confinement paired with purposeful labor. In such institutions, the routine of the day—rise, pray, work, rest—was supposed to fashion order from disarray. It was not merely about keeping people off the streets; it was about teaching them to work, to abide by rules, and to understand the consequences of wrongdoing through the steady rhythm of labor and discipline.

Across the ocean in continental Europe and in the early American towns, similar experiments unfolded, as reformers and officials pressed for a more rational system of punishment. Prisons began to resemble factories in which time itself became a tool of reform. The vocabulary shifted from mere detention to reform, from fear of crime to the possibility of moral retraining. Yet even as these early penological laboratories introduced routine and labor, they also exposed a persistent tension: confinement could degrade as easily as it could discipline. The bodies of prisoners became arenas where power exercised itself daily—through strict schedules, enforced silence, and the moral language of reform that promised a better citizen on the other side of the wall.

The medical and religious sensibilities of the period pushed the idea that crime was not only a legal violation but a personal failing to be corrected. Reformers argued that place mattered—that the physical arrangement of a prison could nurture virtue or exacerbate vice. The result was a cascade of innovations: separate cells, systematic labor, religious instruction, and the inception of official inspections that would later give citizens a voice in the fate of those behind bars.

In this chapter, the story begins with those first brittle assurances that confinement could be more than a cruel necessity. It traces the experiments by which early prisons tried to become moral schools, even as they discovered that power exercised in stone could swiftly harden into its own form of tyranny. The birth of the carceral age was, paradoxically, both a rebellion against arbitrary punishment and a crystallization of it—an assertion that the state could mold souls by the architecture of walls and the cadence of daily life.

THE PENITENTIARY IDEAL

The penitentiary ideal arrived with a bold, unsettling proposition: solitude could reform the soul. In the early 19th century, as penitentiaries rose in the United States and Europe, reformers crafted a language of moral improvement that sounded almost devotional. The goal was not merely to punish criminals but to purify them—to deprive them of companionship and noise until their better natures emerged from within. The first great experiment of this philosophy unfolded at Eastern State Penitentiary in Philadelphia, with its celebrated system of solitary confinement. There, every inmate was placed in a single cell, the walls lined with the quiet of unbroken hours, the only regular conversation being with the chaplain or the warden on Sundays. The architecture was intended to be a cocoon of reform: miles of corridors, a vision of the soul in isolation, as if the mind could be remade by the discipline of silence.

Across the Atlantic, the New York Auburn system offered a striking alternative. It rejected total isolation in favor of congregate work, albeit under a strict regime of silence. Prisoners labored together in factories, yet spoke little, keeping to the ritual of quiet efficiency. The model promised economic efficiency and social control: more workers, lower costs, and a public confidence that discipline was possible in a crowded institution. It was a pragmatic counterpoint to the idealistic solitude of Pennsylvania, a reminder that punishment, even when cloaked in the language of moral reform, remained inseparable from management and control.

The penitentiary era was fueled by a conviction that confinement, properly designed, could alter character. Proponents spoke of moral suasion—the daily opportunity for reflection, confession, and religious instruction—as if the walls themselves could persuade a change of heart. Critics, however, soon pointed to the human costs: the mental strain of isolation, the moral hazard of turning prisoners into hollow shells, and the logistical temptations to expand the reach of punishment through ever-stricter regimes. In the end, the penitentiary ideal was not just about reforming the prisoner; it also tested the state's confidence in its own power to shape the inner life of its citizens, with architecture as a kind of social technology.

WORK AS DISCIPLINE

If the early penitentiaries offered a sanctuary for the soul through silence and solitary routine, the postbellum carceral landscape insisted on something harder: work as discipline, and profit as punishment. The idea was straightforward and brutal: if confinement is to teach, then labor must be the instrument of that teaching—and labor could also subsidize the prison, or even be leased to private employers who needed cheap, controllable labor.

In the United States, this logic produced a grim trifecta: hard labor, chain gangs, and convict leasing. Prisons and jails secularized into industrial operations that assigned inmates to long hours of forced labor in mines, timber camps, road crews, and railroad construction. The chain gang—the long lines of prisoners marching under watchful eyes, often under the lash—became a stark symbol of punishment's economic dimensions. It was not unusual for prisoners to be paid pennies per day for grueling work, with much of the proceeds flowing into the state treasuries or private contracts that profited from the use of convict labor. The labor system entwined punishment with profit, which in turn empowered a racialized regime of punishment in the South after emancipation.

Convict leasing amplified this dynamic. States and counties found it advantageous to lease prisoners to plantations, mines, timber outfits, and even railroad builders. The leasing arrangement meant that the workday's hours and the prisoners' living conditions were set by leaseholders who paid for the labor and bore little of the burden of reform. The result could be brutal, often brutalizing, and it exposed a troubling irony: a society pledged to reforming souls could still profit from the bodies of the imprisoned. Across borderlands and frontier towns, the lines between punishment and profit blurred, and the carceral state found a ready source of labor to fuel industrial expansion and extractive enterprises.

The labor regime also reinforced the central paradox of the carceral age: confinement could discipline, but it could also degrade. The work's intent was to graft civility onto the incarcerated body—to inculcate industrious habits, timeliness, and obedience—yet the social costs could be steep. Labor routines became the visible face of punishment, a material reminder that the state's most intimate power is the power to compel a body to labor. As the century wore on, reformers would challenge not only the conditions inside the walls but the very logic that treated people as a resource to be counted, priced, and put to work.

WOMEN AND CHILDREN BEHIND BARS

Behind the bars of early carceral institutions, gender and age carved separate paths of punishment. Women and children did not simply inhabit the same walls as men; they traveled into prisons with different concerns, fears, and moral logics wrapped around their bodies and lives. For much of the 18th and 19th centuries, female inmates lived in close quarters with men, or in shelters that offered little privacy or dignity. The reform impulse of the era—rooted in ideas about virtue, domesticity, and maternal responsibility—pushed officials to locate women in spaces designed to preserve what whispers of femininity could still be salvaged inside a system designed to break the will.

As men argued about reform, women became both subjects of reform and agents of it. Reformatories and women's prisons emerged with a distinctly gendered design: spaces intended to anthropomorphize virtue and restore moral standing through domestic routines, sewing, laundry, and service work. The gaze of reform often framed women as mothers in need of protection, even when their confinement was born of poverty, crime, or wartime upheaval. The experience of mothers—separated from their children, sometimes kept from visiting rooms and personal shifts in ranks of authority—lay bare a principal moral problem of punishment: when the family is torn apart by the state, can rehabilitation ever be measured as a public good?

Girls and boys, too, found their own specialized places in the carceral system. The emergence of juvenile facilities, reform schools, and other protective spaces sought to shelter younger offenders from the harsher climates of adult prisons. But the line between care and coercion was thin. Juvenile justice would wrestle with questions of consent, culpability, and the degree to which youth could be shaped by confinement. In these gendered and juvenile spheres, punishment transformed into a social project about the family, the future citizen, and the boundaries of state intervention into private life.

Across decades and continents, women, girls, and boys taught the carceral state harsh lessons about who gets protected, who gets punished, and at what cost to the social fabric. The architecture of punishment began to reflect not a single doctrine of reform but a spectrum of assumptions about vulnerability, responsibility, and the proper reach of state power.

SCIENCE MEETS PUNISHMENT

Criminology's flirtation with biology arrived with a provocative claim: crime could be read in the body. Italian writers of the late 19th century argued that criminality was not just a social deviation but a biological inheritance. Cesare Lombroso's famous assertion was that criminals bore detectable physiological traits—atavistic features, facial anomalies, a certain 'stubborn' jaw and pronounced cheekbones—that marked them as biologically predisposed to crime. The field of criminal anthropology gathered momentum as scientists sought to quantify "criminal nature" through skull measurements, photographs, and the measurement of physical attributes. The language was clinical, almost neutral. The implication, however, was anything but neutral: if crime could be read in the body, punishment could be justified as a corrective of an ingrained defect rather than the result of social conditions or personal choice.

Lombroso's ideas gained traction in both Europe and the United States, nurtured by a broader turn toward determinism in the late 19th and early 20th centuries. Other Italian thinkers—Raffaele Garofalo and Enrico Ferri—extended the program, arguing that criminal behavior could be predicted and prevented by addressing individual and social risk factors. The science, however, held a dangerous capacity to justify discrimination. If "born criminals" were a fixed category, then reform could be deemed pointless, and harsh, even inhumane, policies could appear scientifically warranted. As psychologists and psychiatrists joined courts as expert witnesses, the boundary between evidence and inference grew blurred. The era's experiments with psychology tests, mental diagnoses, and the once-dominant belief in fixed criminal types helped unlock a debate about punishment's purpose: were prisons correcting pathology, or were they cultivating it?

The seductive promise of science coincided with darker currents: eugenics, immigration restriction, and social policy built on the assumption that social ills could be traced to biological lineage. The era encouraged experimentation on the bodies and minds of the incarcerated, often with little regard for consent or welfare. Yet even as this science overreached, it provoked counter-movements. Critics asked for more careful attention to environment, to education, to opportunity, and to the social roots of crime. If physical type could not reliably predict criminal behavior, perhaps the real terrain for improvement lay in social reform, education, and opportunity rather than the anatomy of a criminal's skull.

RESISTANCE AND REFORM

The prisons of the carceral age did not simply weather their own failures; they provoked waves of resistance. Reformers traveled from town to town to document conditions, press for better treatment, and insist that punishment could be compatible with humanity. John Howard's meticulous inspections, widely shared through pamphlets and reports, exposed squalor, corruption, and the neglect that accompanied many prisons. His work inspired a generation of inspectors, reformers, and politicians to demand standards, accountability, and a public reckoning with the consequences of confinement. Elizabeth Fry became a visible advocate for women prisoners, delivering a moral not just of compassion but of practical reform: better facilities, more humane treatment, and access to education and religious life for inmates. The public conversation around punishment began to shift as stories of abuse and neglect entered newspapers, sermons, and political debates.

Prison riots, uprisings, and the tireless work of abolitionists and reformers underscored the limits of punitive confinement. The reform movement did not simply want more humane prisons; it sought to reimagine punishment as a system that could serve justice and social welfare rather than simply deter crime. Inspectors, parliamentary commissions, and activist networks built a counter-narrative to the carceral model, one that questioned whether prisons could ever be humane or effective and argued instead for alternative sanctions, probation, and modes of accountability rooted in social support.

The abolitionist impulse—often tied to broader movements for civil rights, labor rights, and humanitarian reform—entered the conversation about who deserves punishment and how to treat the incarcerated as full members of a society with rights and dignities. The tensions between punishment and reform were not resolved in this era; they were intensified. The carceral age, in its early decades, would become a laboratory in which advocates, officials, and inmates themselves pressed for a future in which confinement could be more just, more humane, and more attentive to the possibility of transformation—without ignoring the hard truths about power, race, class, and gender that confinement inevitably enshrined.

SIX

CITIES, COPS, AND COURTS: THE MAKING OF THE MODERN CRIMINAL JUSTICE SYSTEM

FROM NIGHT WATCH TO POLICE FORCE: LONDON, PARIS, AND BEYOND

In crowded streets and on riverbanks where carts clatter and factory whistles scream from dawn to dusk, the modern idea of policing did not arrive with a single trumpet blast. It arrived as a slow shuffle of reforms, controversies, and learned arguments about how to balance liberty with safety. If you wanted to read the origins of the contemporary police, you could start much earlier than most people expect—with the night watch and the scribbled notes of magistrates, with the early, rudimentary forms of municipal order that preceded the modern state in many European capitals.

In London, the transformation began as a hybrid of habit and experiment. Before the Metropolitan Police Act of

1829, the city relied on watchmen who kept different hours, paid piecemeal, and answered to local magistrates who often knew the neighborhoods well but could not scale to the city's growing needs. The Bow Street Runners, active in the mid-18th century under Henry Fielding, are often remembered as the first professional foils to crime in a modern city, though they remained informal relative to what would come next. They operated on the edge of legality, employing informers, cracking cases that required a swift, organized response, and combining social influence with a handful of constables who wore something that looked like authority but did not yet look like a national institution.

Paris followed a parallel arc, but with distinct political ambitions. The city's police world had long been tangled with the needs of empire, revolution, and crowd control. In the first half of the 19th century, urban reforms began to mature under a shifting regime that needed order but also had to manage citizen dissent. The institution responsible for this work grew more formal: the city's policing authority, the prefect of police, began to centralize authority, establish regular patrols, and create the kind of network that could track crime across blocks rather than across parishes. A parallel development darkened the horizon: the creation of the Sûreté and its later expansion into a more systematic force able to gather intelligence, run investigations, and operate beyond simple night watch duties. Uniforms appeared, communication networks expanded, and the idea of surveillance became respectable rather than ominous—a transformation that allowed the state to project power while promising the public a predictable routine of safety.

In both cities, the logic of centralized policing met fierce pushback. Critics warned that a standing force would become a blunt instrument of political control, eroding civil liberties, enabling indiscriminate surveillance, and muzzling dissent. Supporters argued that crime in rapidly expanding urban spaces demanded professional eyes and trained hands—people who could keep pace with street gangs, commercial fraud, and the logistical chaos of dense populations. The debate was not merely about crime; it was about what kind of society the authorities claimed to govern. Was the police a servant of the people, a guardian of common safety, or a tool for the ruling class to chill public agitation?

A shift in the balance of power followed the innovations of the early 19th century. Police officers began to patrol in uniform, marking a visible presence that signaled not intimidation alone but a predictable order. The force slowly turned into a bureaucracy, with rules, ranks, and standard duties. It was not instantaneous, and it was not universally welcomed, but it was inarguably durable. The transformation did not erase crime; it reframed it as a problem for the state to manage systematically. The question that haunted every reform was the same one that limits every modern police force: how to police without turning public life into a ledger of fear. The answers would continue to evolve as cities grew, technologies changed, and new kinds of crime emerged. And with that evolution came a new science of crime control that would define policing for generations to come.

CRIME IN THE INDUSTRIAL CITY: CROWDS, GANGS, AND NEW ANXIETIES

The nineteenth century turned cities into living machines. Steel, glass, and brick pressed against the old social orders, and crime responded in kind. In the new urban centers, crime did not disappear; it transformed. The crowded streets, the tenements stacked like matchboxes, and the factory districts at the edge of town created a texture of life in which danger could seem to lurk around every corner. Police reformers and social reformers often spoke a common language about the dangers of modernity: anonymity, alienation, and the inadequate supervision of masses.

In these cities, crime took on a new face. It became less a handful of bold outlaws and more a system of street economies and organized mischief conducted by groups who exploited the dense, impersonal nature of the metropolis. Crowds gathered at markets, stations, and public squares, and the very density that fed commerce also amplified risk. Pickpockets learned to blend into streams of pedestrians; street sellers integrated with the crowd to harvest wallets and pockets. Urban myths grew quickly—panics about mobs and riots that could swell from a minor dispute into a citywide crisis in a matter of hours. The fear was not merely about losing possessions; it was about losing order itself.

Gangs emerged as a response to these pressures. They provided a rough sense of belonging, a shared economy, and a predictable code of conduct in an environment where traditional social ties frayed. The debates about these groups sharpened as reformers pressed for a more professionalized force to separate legitimate enterprise from criminal enterprise, to distinguish the desperate from the dangerous, and to locate the culprits without turning whole neighborhoods into suspects. The vocabulary of crime—the "criminal class," the social pathology of urban life—became a staple of political rhetoric, even as real people lived in the daily tension of crowded streets, noisy factories, and late-night transit.

Public health concerns often braided with crime concerns. Cholera, typhus, and poor sanitation created a sense that danger did not come solely from intentional wrongdoing. It came from the environment itself. The city was both a laboratory for progress and a stage where fear could be exploited. In this climate, officials looked for answers in planning, surveillance, and a more predictable legal framework. They sought to answer the question not only of how to catch criminals but how to reduce the incentives for crime in the first place. The result was a growing belief that crime could be managed—if not eliminated—through a combination of deterrent punishment, social services, and institutional efficiency. It was the beginning of a broader policy project that would continue to define modern criminal justice for generations: crime as a problem of systems, not just individuals.

DETECTIVES AND THE BIRTH OF CRIMINAL INVESTIGATION

If policing in the early industrial city was about walking the beat and maintaining a public presence, the late nineteenth century brought a new kind of craft: the detective. The police already had a reputation for chasing what was obvious—the visible crime in the street—while the world of serious wrongdoing required a more patient, methodical approach. Detectives emerged as specialists who could track patterns, gather clues, and connect seemingly unrelated elements in a case. It was an era hungry for certainty, and detectives promised it in the form of carefully built stories: timelines, alibis, witnesses, and a chain of evidence that could stand up in court.

The birth of the detective in this period was as much about institutional growth as it was about popular imagination. London's Metropolitan Police, Paris's urban reformers, and other major cities built dedicated districts whose job was to pursue the "why" behind the crime, not merely the "who." The detective's toolbox expanded with new techniques. The careful collection of fingerprints began to enter the mainstream during the late nineteenth century, and with it, the idea that the fingerprint could identify a person with a nearly perfect reliability. For the first time, investigators could lean on physical traces rather than pure inference. Witness interviews became formal procedures, and case files grew into databases of sorts—compilations of small details that required meticulous organization.

The public imagination also helped to shape this professional identity. The detective, once a romantic figure in penny-plain stories, achieved something closer to a modern archetype: patient, relentless, and almost surgical in its precision. The press contributed to the myth, chasing "greatest feats of deduction" and sensationalizing the still-new science of investigation. Yet behind the romance lay a practical shift: investigation was no longer the exclusive domain of magistrates and confidents but a specialized skill set within the police. The detective's rise signaled a broader transformation of the justice system—from reacting to crime to anticipating it, from securing confessions through coercion to building cases through careful analysis and boring but indispensable paperwork.

PROFESSIONALIZING JUSTICE: LAWYERS, JUDGES, AND LEGAL TRAINING

As cities industrialized and the state expanded its reach, the machinery of justice grew more organized, more predictable, and more expensive. The courtroom became a space not only for deciding guilt or innocence but for demonstrating that the system itself could be fair. This meant a professionalization of the people who worked there: lawyers trained in formal methods, judges who presided over routine procedures, and clerks who kept meticulous records. The legal professions expanded in step with the expansion of the state, and with that expansion came a shift in power. The courtroom moved from a local, personal arena to a more bureaucratic, standardized process capable of handling larger volumes of cases.

In many places the training of lawyers and judges changed in tandem with reforms in legal education. Law libraries grew, schools affiliated with universities began to grant degrees in law, and the old networks of influence began to yield to formal credentials. The practice of law became more technical: the cross-examination, the presentation of evidence, and the arguments about procedure framed how guilt could be established and how justice could be administered fairly. Trials began to look more like debates with a set of rational rules than public spectacles of passion. This change did not eliminate controversy; it reframed it. Debates about the balance between speed and accuracy, about the rights of the accused, and about the proper role of lawyers in the process persisted and deepened.

At the same time, the relationship between police and prosecutors intensified. The professionalization of justice created a faith in the prosecutorial function as the engine of criminal accountability. Prosecutors rose as political actors, bureaucrats who could navigate the complexities of case management, evidence standards, and institutional priorities. The courtroom itself became a site of reform as standards of proof, rules of evidence, and procedures for ensuring fair trial were debated, revised, and sometimes reshaped. In many places, this era also bred a degree of optimism about reform: if the system could be codified, if the lawyers and judges could learn to think in terms of rights and proportionality, perhaps punishment could be refined rather than simply extended. Yet the work of professionalizing justice was inseparable from the broader social and political project of the age, which used law to organize power in an urbanizing world.

COLONIAL POLICING: EMPIRE, RACE, AND CONTROL AT A DISTANCE

Policing did not stay within the borders of the metropolis. The same institutions that trained and disciplined officers at home were transplanted to far-flung corners of empires, where they confronted unfamiliar landscapes, languages, and populations. If the nineteenth century taught cities how to manage crowds, it also demonstrated how to manage peoples who were ruled rather than born into a social contract. Colonial policing was, in part, a testing ground for the techniques and theories that would later be used inland in the metropoles, but it was also a profound assertion of power at a distance.

Across continents, policing carried the heavy burden of empire. In places like India, Africa, the Caribbean, and the Pacific, policing regimes blended local informants, colonial administrators, and a growing class of professional law enforcers. The result was a system that could respond quickly to urban disturbances and political uprisings, but it did so through a lens of racial hierarchy and political control. The architecture of the legal system—what counted as a crime, who could be prosecuted, how trials were conducted—often reflected imperial priorities: the suppression of dissent, the extraction of resources, and the maintenance of order as a claim of governance. The law could appear as a neutral instrument, but it operated alongside a web of power that included forced labor, surveillance networks, and punitive sanctions aimed at communities seen as troublesome or unreliable.

Colonial policing also reshaped the practice of law back home. Officers trained in the colonies brought back new ideas about intelligence gathering, anti-riot tactics, and the management of large, diverse populations. The line between policing for public safety and policing for control could blur easily. In some cases, colonial experiences pushed reforms that would later inform domestic policing in the metropole; in others, they left a troubling blueprint for the expansion of surveillance and coercion. Either way, the imperial project of policing proved that the question of who counts as a citizen—and who is treated as a threat—was not a fixed moral category. It was something that was negotiated, across borders and across centuries, through policy, practice, and the continual rewriting of what a crime is and what a punishment demands.

CRIME STORIES AND PUBLIC OPINION: NEWSPAPERS, PENNY DREADFULS, AND PANICS

If the police built the machinery of order, the media supplied the soundtrack. The nineteenth century saw the rise of mass circulation newspapers, sensational pamphlets, and the legendary penny dreadfuls—cheap, exciting stories about crime, villains, and daring do. Crime became not just an event but a narrative, a thing that could be told in dramatic headlines and illustrated with lurid engravings. The public consumed these stories at a pace that rivaled the speed of a train, and the more dramatic the tale, the more it circulated. This was a period when the public footprint of crime could grow as quickly as the crime itself, shaping opinions and influencing policy in real time.

The relationship between crime reporting and policy was symbiotic. Vivid reportage could swell public fear and push for harsher punishment, while reformers could cite media attention as evidence of social breakdown requiring intervention. The press helped create a shared cultural language about crime—criminals were not simply wrongdoers but symbols of danger to the social order. The effect was double-edged. On one hand, journalism publicized injustices, exposed corruption, and spurred reforms that improved fairness in the courts and the treatment of suspects. On the other hand, sensationalism could distort perception: a single notorious case could become a blueprint for panic, and a villain's profile could crowd out nuanced understanding of social causes such as poverty, inequality, and political repression.

Penny dreadfuls and sensational crime writing also fed the imagination of professional detectives and state investigators. The romanticized figure of the sleuth—calm, clever, and almost superhuman in deduction—captured the public imagination and helped ordinary readers understand crime as a puzzle that could be solved with the right method. It encouraged readers to accept the idea that insights, followed by careful procedure, would bring criminals to justice. Yet the stories also reminded readers of the limits of the new system: there were countless cases where the evidence was ambiguous, the motives murky, and the moral arithmetic not so clear. As newspapers multiplied and the public's appetite for crime stories grew, a new cycle of fear, reform, and inquiry took root: crime would be reported, policies would be debated, and the pendulum between punishment and protection would swing again and again.

SEVEN

SCIENCE IN THE DOCK: FORENSICS, PSYCHOLOGY, AND THE CRIMINAL MIND

TRACING IDENTITIES: PASSPORTS AND PRINTS

For centuries, knowing who stood before you mattered as much as knowing what they had done. Names could be borrowed, alliances shifted, and bodies moved across borders like ships in a harbor. Yet the modern state needed something steadier than memory and rumor. It needed a way to identify the nameless, tag the unknown, and trace someone who vanished into the crowd. Identification would become an instrument of power, and fingerprints, not fealties, would prove decisive in law's long march from suspicion to evidence.

In the late nineteenth century a French police officer named Alphonse Bertillon proposed a systematic solution to a stubborn problem: how to tell one offender from another when names on paper could be wrong, and aliases could fool a district attorney. His answer was bertillonage, a careful catalog of measurements—head length, ear position, arm span—supplemented by scales of bodily marks. It looked scientific. It sounded reliable. And in practice it often failed. A misrecorded measurement, a mistaken tape, or a single innocent body whose features coincidentally resembled another's could lock a person into a case file for months or years. The system worked best for a time and then collided with the messy randomness of human bodies.

A turning point arrived with an unlikely pair of glimpses into the future: a stubbornly durable question about whether a person could be identified by a map of the skin rather than a map of the bone. The idea of fingerprinting —of noting the minute, unique patterns that every person bears on their fingertips—gained traction after a thread of discovery. In the 1890s scientists like Sir Francis Galton and independent contributors around the world argued that fingerprints were unique and immutable, a tiny natural barcode for each person. Meanwhile, in places far from Paris, practitioners like Juan Vucetich and Edward Henry (in Britain) refined classification systems that could turn a messy print into a workable lead in a crowded courtroom.

The breakthrough was not only scientific; it was bureaucratic. In 1901 the United Kingdom adopted a standardized fingerprint classification scheme, and the method spread to police departments across the empire and beyond. A decade later the United States began to rely more on fingerprints than on the Bertillon measurements that had once seemed so definitive. Then came a dramatic demonstration of the limits of name-based identification. In 1903 a case from Leavenworth prison, often summarized as the Will West story, exposed the hollowness of many human-made identifiers. Two inmates shared the same name, the same age, even the same physical description. Only after fingerprinting did authorities realize one of them was an entirely different man. The lesson was simple and brutal: if you want to know who did something, you must know who they are, down to the unique pattern of their skin.

The state's reach did not stop at prisons; it began to regulate movement itself. Passports and identity papers, once a courtesy of travelers and merchants, grew to become tools of border control. In the busy world of cities and ports, officials needed stable records—birth registers, civil certificates, photographs, and, increasingly, biometrics—to decide who could cross, whose testimony would be trusted, and who might pose a risk to others. The fingerprint, then, was not just a forensic tool; it became a social technology, a way to translate a person into a verifiable code that could travel across time and territory.

With the rise of the photograph in law enforcement and the standardization of identification, the stage was set for a broader architecture of proof. Mugshots filled files alongside fingerprints; police notebooks stacked beside citizen registries; and the aura of science began to drape even the most practical acts—checking a passport at a harbor, matching a print at a crime scene, linking a suspect to a case through a single invisible line that only a specialist could read.

Yet the story of identification is not a triumphal march. It reveals a recurring tension: the more we rely on standardized measures to identify people, the more we expose ourselves to error, bias, and the illusion that a fingerprint is a fingerprint of truth. The later chapters of science in the dock will remind us that even the sharpest tools require judgment, safeguards, and humility. Identification can unlock doors and convict the innocent; it can also be manipulated or misunderstood. The art is to know when a pattern is meaningful and when it is merely a clue that demands careful, responsible interpretation.

THE LAB AS EVIDENCE FACTORY

The idea that science could turn traces into confident conclusions traveled unevenly from laboratories to courts, but it gathered momentum with every new facility and every new instrument. The early laboratories of forensic science did not appear all at once. They emerged from a confluence of curiosity, professional ambition, and the stubborn insistence that law could be tested against the facts of the natural world. The spark was ignited by

Edmond Locard, whose Lyon laboratory became a touchstone for a practical creed: evidence is a conversation between the scene and the observer. If something left the scene, something else must have entered it. The exchange principle—that the guilty party and the crime scene exchange material with one another—provided a lucid, repeatable, and testable way to conceptualize a mystery.

In the years that followed, cities and nations built their own houses of science for crime. The laboratory was no longer a hidden corner of a police station; it was a dedicated space—sleek, orderly, and scientific—where stains, fibers, and fragments could be coaxed into stories. Blood typing, once a stubborn puzzle, opened a window into who had bled and who had bled whom. The ABO blood groups discovered by Karl Landsteiner in the early twentieth century offered a practical filter: a blood sample could exclude many suspects even when it could not pin a culprit with absolute certainty. The lab's medicines were not miracle cures but reliable probabilities, the kind of cautious inference that a juror could understand if explained clearly.

The rise of forensic laboratories also meant a new kind of specialization. Ballistics experts learned to read the marks left by weapons on bullets and cartridges, disentangling the choreography of a crime from the chaos of a scene. Specialists in trace evidence—fibers, glass, soil, and pollen—began to reconstruct journeys as minute as a fiber in a glove or a fragment of fabric on a sleeve. Document examiners learned to separate authentic handwriting from counterfeit squiggles, a task as much about psychology as chemistry. The laboratory transformed crime from a matter of luck and guesswork into a disciplined interrogation of physical truth.

But science is never perfect, and the laboratory's authority is not the same as law's certainty. If a hair found at a scene seems to match a suspect under a microscope, a prosecutor may still need to bridge the gap from correlation to causation. The chain of custody, the calibration of instruments, and the quality of the sample all matter. The modern lab is a place of promise and peril: it can illuminate a path to justice, but it can also mislead if its methods are misused or misunderstood. The courtroom, in turn, must temper expectation with critical appraisal, asking whether a result speaks to guilt beyond reasonable doubt or merely narrows the field of suspects to a single plausible candidate.

TO THE EDGE OF REASON: WHY INSANITY MATTERS

Throughout history, the law has wrestled with a stubborn paradox: how to punish a person who is not fully in control of their actions? The question of insanity sits at the boundary between medicine and law, between compassion and protection, between the fairest judgment and the cruelest harm. The courtroom's encounter with mental illness is not a single event but a long conversation, shifting in tone as ideas about cognition, accountability, and the mind's fragility change.

The M'Naghten rule, established in 1843 after a famous British case, became a lodestar for many legal systems. It argued that a defendant could not be held responsible if, at the time of the act, they were laboring under a defect of reason so as not to know the nature and quality of the act, or if they did know it, they did not know that what they were doing was wrong. This standard placed emphasis on cognitive awareness, rather than emotional or volitional impairment. It provided a clear test, but it also prompted new questions: what does it mean to know wrong from right when the mind itself misreads right from wrong?

As the century turned, courts explored other ways of framing mental illness in relation to crime. The irresistable impulse test allowed for exculpation if a person could not resist a sudden urge. The Durham rule offered a broader, more permissive standard that permitted criminal responsibility to hinge on whether the act was the product of mental disease. In the mid-twentieth century, many jurisdictions shifted again, influenced by progressive thoughts about rehabilitation, freedom from excessive punishment, and the idea that punishment should fit neither cruelty nor mere misfortune alone.

Psychiatry's role in the courtroom grew into a science of its own, a clinical language that could translate private experience into public accountability. Expert witnesses described delusions, compulsions, and the consequences of brain injury; juries listened for a diagnosis, a prognosis, and an explanation that could connect motive with responsibility. But this role carried risk. Psychiatric experts could be wrong, biased, or overconfident. The judge's question shifted from whether a person committed a crime to whether the person's mind could be said to bear moral fault. For every breakthrough in understanding a motive or mental state, there remained a counterargument about fairness and the duty to protect the vulnerable while safeguarding the public.

In a sense, insanity testing is a barometer for how a society balances knowledge with mercy. If science can illuminate the workings of a troubled mind, it can also tempt courts to replace moral judgment with clinical certainty. The decades that followed would push these tensions into ever more public debates—from neuropsychiatry to courtroom governance—reminding us that the mind's deepest mysteries are not only medical problems but social tests of justice.

MIND OVER MATTER: MEASURING MINDS AND MORAL WORTH

The late nineteenth and early twentieth centuries brought a wave of ideas that crime could be explained, and perhaps cured, through measurements of intellect, temperament, and heredity. The notion of degeneracy—an idea that criminality could be inherited or tied to a deficient character—captured the imaginations of reformers and authorities alike. It sounded scientific, even humane: if we could identify the seeds of crime, we could plant the conditions for prevention. But the seedbeds they cultivated often bore toxic fruit.

In the shadow of eugenics movements, many scholars argued that certain traits—feeble-mindedness, impulsivity, susceptibility to crime—were in some sense quantifiable and passably improveable or, in harsher formulations, fixable by social engineering. The work of people like Cesare Lombroso, who spoke of the "atavistic" criminal as a throwback to primitive humanity, reinforced the belief that some people were born to offend. American and European reformers embraced similar notions and pressed for policies that today seem unconscionable: segregation, restrictive immigration rules, and the sterilization of those deemed biologically unfit. The courts, tragically, sometimes acted as if these scientific theories settled who deserved liberty and who should be controlled.

IQ testing arrived as the twentieth century matured. The idea that intelligence could be measured numerically offered a seductive clarity: a single score might decide a person's fate in education, employment, and, yes, crime. But the tests were not neutral. They reflected cultural assumptions, language barriers, and class biases that favored those already advantaged. In some jurisdictions, high scores could be weaponized to label a person as less human, more dangerous, or less likely to reform. In others, low scores justified harsher treatment, including segregation or coercive education.

As the century wore on, the science grew more sophisticated even as its moral weather changed. Brain imaging, neuropsychological testing, and a growing catalog of behavioral traits offered new ways to talk about risk and responsibility. Yet the core problem remained stubbornly human: how to reconcile the desire to understand the criminal mind with the duty to treat people justly. The era's loudest claims often masked a deeper truth—science can illuminate patterns, but it can also be used to justify inequality. The challenge for courts, scholars, and citizens was to demand humility from the science and compassion from the system.

THE LAB'S DARK SIDE AND THE PROMISE OF TRUTH

If laboratories promise clarity, the courtroom must judge how much certainty is enough to convict. In the second half of the twentieth century, science in the dock faced a fierce test: how to translate laboratory certainty into legal certainty. The same pulse of confidence that makes a DNA analysis seem airtight can become a trap when method and interpretation are misapplied. This tension is

SCIENCE IN THE DOCK: FORENSICS, PSYCHOLOGY, AN... 93

not a modern invention; it has always been part of the chemistry between science and law.

One of science's hardest lessons is that measurement is not revelation; it is interpretation wrapped in numbers. The same strand of hair under a microscope can be described with impressive precision, yet the question remains: does it prove guilt, or merely place a suspect at the scene? The same fingerprint pattern can be compared to a database with extraordinary specificity, but a single misstep in collection, labeling, or analysis can tilt the verdict toward wrongfulness or mercy.

These concerns have produced both safeguards and scandals. The safeguards include standardized protocols for evidence collection, blind verification of results, and a clear chain of custody that follows every item from scene to courtroom. The scandals have often involved overconfident conclusions from tests that lacked sufficient validation, or specialized disciplines that sounded scientific but were not yet ready for courtroom scrutiny. Bite-mark analysis, for example, became popular in some courts before a robust consensus existed about its reliability, leading to wrongful convictions and later exonerations.

The high-stakes drama of scientific evidence has also sparked reforms. The courts have increasingly demanded that experts explain not just what their data show, but how they know what they know. They ask for reproducibility, peer review, and an explicit articulation of limitations. The result is a three-way conversation: scientists describe the data; lawyers translate them into legal meaning; judges provide the standard by which evidence passes or fails. When it works well, science clarifies questions that law alone cannot answer. When it falters, it can overturn the most confident claim with a hard, corrective truth: the human stakes exceed the certainty of any instrument.

PROFILING THE UNKNOWN: CRIME, CLUES, AND THE ART OF PREDICTION

The late twentieth century brought a different kind of scientific enthusiasm to the dock: the hope that behavior could be read like a text, that the pattern of a crime scene could tell us the shape of its author. Serial murders, media spectacles, and a growing fear of the unknown offender created fertile ground for profiling. The FBI's Behavioral Analysis Unit began to systematically study case files, gather interviews, and build a language for describing patterns of behavior. The idea was not to guess a name but to narrow the field of suspects by describing the likely characteristics of the perpetrator.

Profiling emerged from a mix of criminology, psychology, and a storytelling impulse. Investigators described the entry, the method, the signature, and the victim's story. They mapped motives, opportunities, and means, seeking a psychological fingerprint that could guide investigators toward the most promising leads. In popular culture the profiler became a new hero, simultaneously celebrated for insight and criticized for uncertainty. The truth was messier than the narrative suggested: profiles could be evocative and help guide interviews, yet they were not a substitute for solid evidence. They could lead investigators to the right person—or the wrong one—if taken as gospel rather than as one piece of the puzzle.

The tools of profiling also reflected a broader shift in how we think about risk. The science of behavioral prediction borrowed from statistics, psychology, and criminology to forecast danger in a way that could feel almost prescient. But the more we rely on predictions, the more we invite bias, misinterpretation, and the danger of turning a suspect's future into their fate. Profiling unsettled the idea that criminals are timeless types and crimes are isolated events; it pushed us toward a more subtle map of human behavior, one that recognizes variability, context, and the limits of what we can know about another person's mind.

EIGHT
WAR, REVOLUTION, AND DICTATORSHIP: CRIME AND PUNISHMENT IN EXTREMES

TOTAL WAR AND EMERGENCY POWERS: WHEN SECURITY TRUMPS RIGHTS

In the ash and pelt of modern conflict, the line between justice and emergency becomes dangerously thin. The state speaks in a louder voice during total war, and that voice often drowns out the individual citizen. Curfews flicker across cities like red warning signs. Newspapers are censored, radio broadcasts filtered, and leaders claim that times of crisis demand exceptional measures. The idea that "all is fair in war" has a stubborn way of slipping from rhetoric into policy. What counts as a crime shifts when the enemy is everywhere and nowhere at once; suspicion becomes a legitimate weapon, and the old rules about due process and proportionality retreat under the pressure of danger.

During World War I and World War II, governments stretched the law to cover acts that would otherwise be criminal, or treated crimes as not crimes at all when they served the war effort. The machinery of the state—police, courts, intelligence services—was given new powers to detain, censor, surveil, and punish. Habeas corpus was suspended in many places, mail and telegraph lines were monitored, and so-called "emergency acts" piled up like a defensive shield around the state. In some cases, this meant crackdowns on political opponents, in others, broad surveillance of whole communities deemed risks to national security. The crime of dissent could be met with administrative coercion rather than a criminal trial; counterweights to authority were converted into legitimizing routines of control.

The logic is chillingly straightforward: if the regime proclaims that the survival of the state is at stake, then any transgression that aids survival becomes a permissible target of punishment. In practice this meant that laws themselves could be weaponized. The crime became not merely illegal acts but any acts that undermined the war effort, the homeland, or national unity. Prosecutions could be turned into acts of public theater designed to intimidate, reassure, or unify. The courtroom could function as a stage where the state demonstrates to its people and to the world that it is in command, that danger is real, and that it has answers—harsh, swift, and certain.

The effect on ordinary life was profound. People learned to monitor their own words and gestures, to mistrust their neighbors, to accept intrusive scrutiny as a normal condition of being a citizen. Dissenters—whether political opponents, minority communities, labor activists, or artists whose voices threatened the official line—could be defined as enemies of the state, and thus criminal. The law, in this telling, is not a neutral instrument of justice but a flexible tool of political survival. Punishment becomes a political resource, as much a weapon as a prison or a propaganda broadcast. The shadow of punitive power lengthens and shapes every daily decision—from where to work to what to say in private rooms.

These emergency measures rarely disappear with the end of hostilities. Some endure as part of a state's enduring toolkit, reconstituted and repackaged for new disguises: counterterrorism laws, anti-dissidence campaigns, and mass surveillance programs. Others leave behind scars that persist in the collective memory and frame later debates about security, freedom, and accountability. What lessons emerge from this history? That the power to punish at scale is inseparable from the power to define who qualifies as a legitimate target. That fear, rightly or wrongly, can become the most durable ally of the state's punitive impulse. And that the true question of war's aftermath is not only who loses lives, but how the law itself changes to accommodate the new normal of danger.

As we move to the next section, we step inside the theatre of the state's most deliberate, public forms of punishment: show trials where justice and spectacle intertwine, and where the courtroom becomes a stage for enforcing political will. These trials reveal how regimes use law not merely to convict individuals, but to confirm a narrative of total fidelity to the regime and the ideology it embodies.

POLITICAL CRIMES AND SHOW TRIALS: JUSTICE AS SPECTACLE IN DICTATORSHIPS

If total war creates a climate in which rights are bent toward security, show trials press that bending into a dramatic, public ritual. In dictatorships, the courtroom is less a search for truth than a stage on which power performs its own legitimacy. The defendants may be real individuals, but the charges are sometimes crafted as symbols of a larger threat—internal enemies, traitors, conspirators—whose punishment will prove that the regime is vigilant, decisive, and unyielding. The logic is simple and unnerving: to deter, to discredit, to consolidate control, a public confession and a public verdict must be manufactured.

Stalin's USSR offers one of the most infamous patterns of the show trial. The process is slow, the rhetoric is solemn, and the results are predetermined. A verdict is announced before the hearing begins; the record is designed to entertain every plausible fear: treason, espionage, sabotage. The defendant's role is to perform remorse and loyalty in equal measure, to confess the misdeeds yearned by the regime and to vow fidelity to the future. The interior theater of the trial—the way the prosecutor's questions are scripted, the way the audience's gaze travels from the bench to the crowd, the way the judge intones the sentence with calculable gravity—serves to validate a political order rather than to uncover truth. The law becomes a ritual offering to the state's need for purity of allegiance.

Fascist regimes and other authoritarian states adopt a parallel posture. They cast dissent as a dangerous conspiracy that must be rooted out to preserve the social order. Rule by fear requires a spectacle of culpability that justifies coercion: confessions wrung under pressure, testimonies that pin blame on broad, often bureaucratically dehumanized categories of enemies, and sentences designed to awe the polity into obedience. The specifics differ—from the theater of the courtroom to the choreography of the crowd—but the underlying aim remains the same: to convert law into propaganda, to render justice into a tool for political control, and to show that the regime's power to define crime is the regime's power to define reality.

The consequences reach far beyond the convicted. Families carry the stigma of charges whispered in corridors. Colleagues hesitate to speak freely, fear seeping into casual conversation. The state's credibility rests on its ability to present a seamless narrative of unity and danger, a narrative that compels belief even when the evidence is manufactured or withheld. Over time, such trials imprint a habit of fear into the social fabric: people learn to anticipate punishment, to confess when questioned, to trust only the official line.

Studying these trials helps us understand why regimes prioritize control over rule of law that is accountable to the citizen. It shows how the instrument of justice can be tuned to produce fear, obedience, and the erasure of dissent, all in the name of saving the state. The next section turns to a different, but equally grim instrument of coercion: the camps and gulags, the place where the body and the social order are rearranged through labor, deprivation, and the stark arithmetic of confinement.

CAMPS AND GULAGS: MASS INCARCERATION AS STATE POLICY

Camps and gulags mark a different logic of punishment than the courtroom drama of show trials. Here the aim is not merely to convict or intimidate; it is to transform and exhaust a population through forced labor and deliberate deprivation. The carceral state becomes a vast, asymmetrical project in social engineering, designed to extract value from bodies while breaking spirits. In this regime, punishment is not a sentence handed down to a singular offender. It is a structural condition of life for thousands, sometimes millions, of people who become disappearances written into a system of control.

In one historical orbit, the Soviet Gulag system binds punishment to production. Prisoners are assigned to mines, forests, factories, and railways, compelled to work under conditions that destroy the body long before the court's formal verdict matters. Compulsory labor becomes a source of national strength, turning punishment into an economic instrument as much as a repressive one. The daily life inside the camps features a brutal routine: long hours of exhausting labor, meager rations, overcrowded and unsanitary quarters, brutal discipline, and the survival calculus that inmates learn quickly if they want to endure another week, another month, another sentence. The moral geography of punishment shifts from the courtroom to the work yard, where the punishment is inseparable from the day's labor, from the hunger that gnaws, and from the fear of being chosen for the next shift or the next shift's selection.

The Nazi concentration camps present a more genocidal form of incarceration, where confinement itself doubles as annihilation. Beyond forced labor, thousands were murdered in gas chambers, starved in blocks, subjected to experiments, or deliberately killed through systematic neglect. The state's ideology—racial purity, political obedience, total domination—was engineered into the camp's architecture and routine. The camp is a morbid algorithm: assign a number, strip a person of identity, regulate each day with fear, and let the system do the work of erasure.

The reach of mass incarceration extends beyond the extreme cases of Stalinist and Nazi regimes. Other states use internment camps, political prisons, and forced labor as a means of stabilizing power, signaling that dissent will be crushed and that loyalty is the currency of survival. The consequences reverberate through generations: families fractured by disappearances, communities traumatized by the knowledge that the state can reach into daily life and convert a neighbor into a statistic. The social fabric twists under the weight of confinement, and the memory of such confinement can haunt political culture for decades.

As we move forward, the idea of crime evolves into a broader moral question—how does a society define crimes committed by the state itself or by persons acting under its orders? The next section addresses one of the most morally wrenching chapters of modern law: the attempt to name, categorize, and punish the worst crimes committed by states—the crimes against humanity and genocide that demand a new, shared legal vocabulary.

GENOCIDE AND CRIMES AGAINST HUMANITY: NUREMBERG AND BEYOND

The postwar moment demanded a reckoning that could not be contained within national borders. The Nuremberg Trials did not invent the idea of crimes against humanity, but they codified a new legal norm: certain acts, committed in the name of state policy, are so egregious that the international community bears a collective responsibility to address them. The courtroom in Nuremberg became a stage not only for the individual accused but for a new standard of memory: the crimes of the state that could no longer be treated as the state's private misfortune. Genocide—the deliberate attempt to erase a people—was named and prosecuted, not as a mere violation of a treaty, but as a crime against humanity that demands universal jurisdiction. The meaning of justice stretched beyond national innocence or guilt; it claimed a shared duty to remember, document, and respond to atrocity.

The charge sheet in Nuremberg rested on three pillars: the laws of war, crimes against humanity, and the complicity of leaders who orchestrated or enabled mass murder. The proceedings indicated a crucial shift in international law: if a state commits acts on a grand scale, its claims to sovereignty are compromised by the moral imperative to intervene in some form. The trials did not erase all ambiguity—many victims were left without redress, many perpetrators escaped punishment, and the mechanics of global power politics often impeded a perfect accounting. Yet they planted a seed: that a collective memory of crimes, and a legal framework to respond to them, could endure beyond the collapse of empires and the fall of regimes.

As the century progressed, additional mass atrocities tested and refined the legal vocabulary. Rwanda's genocide and the Balkan conflicts in the 1990s pushed human rights advocates to articulate anew the concepts of responsibility and accountability. The establishment of international tribunals, and the drafting of the Rome Statute that created the International Criminal Court, signaled a global ambition: to deter future atrocity through law, to punish through due process, and to acknowledge victims through truth-telling and reparations. The law, in these moments, attempts to transcend the sovereignty of wrongdoers and to restrain the worst impulses of power. Yet the work remains unfinished. Jurisdiction, evidence, and political will intersect in complex ways, and the victory of formal justice is not guaranteed when political will falters, or when powerful actors rewrite history to shield themselves.

The study of genocide and crimes against humanity thus becomes a mirror for societies in every era: a reminder that the most profound violations of human rights are often committed by those who claim to protect the people. The next section examines how regimes seek to control not only acts but thoughts, fears, and loyalties—how spies, subversives, and secret police manufacture a culture of suspicion that corrodes trust and corrodes civil society.

SPIES, SUBVERSIVES, AND SECRET POLICE: SURVEILLANCE UNDER AUTHORITARIAN RULE

Surveillance is the quiet architecture of every authoritarian order. When the state cannot rule openly through the ballot and the street, it rules through information—who you are, whom you know, what you think, and with whom you speak. Secret police and informant networks make fear a daily habit. The discipline of a society becomes a practice of self-policing, as people learn to anticipate punishments that may arrive in whispers, not courts. The crime grows from a suspicion—an accusation that a person is not wholly loyal to the regime—and it is punished not only for concrete acts but for the potential to commit them. In this climate, the boundary between private life and public surveillance dissolves, and ordinary life becomes a field of risk management.

Consider the image of a surveillance state where an invisible chorus of informants reports every perceived deviation. The secret police cultivate a culture of denunciation, where a neighbor's rumor about political disloyalty can set into motion a cascade of investigations, interrogations, and punitive actions. In such systems, the search for enemies becomes a perpetual project; the state argues that constant vigilance prevents catastrophe. The crime, then, is often not a tangible act but a category—subversive, dissident, unreliable—and punishment aims to rebind individuals to the imagined social purity of the regime. The machinery is enormous: phone taps, mail checks, travel controls, and a sprawling file system that links families, schools, workplaces, and communities into a single net of scrutiny.

The human costs are immense. People are harassed at work, denied housing or travel, and stripped of jobs for supposed disloyalty. The social climate darkens as trust between neighbors erodes. Intellectual life shrinks under the weight of fear, and once-vital public space—the street, the meeting hall, the classroom—becomes a contested domain where loyalty is not just expected but policed. The state's security apparatus thus becomes not only a weapon against real or imagined enemies but a tool that shapes how people think, speak, and form associations.

In looking at these regimes, we carry forward a crucial question: what is justice when the instrument of control can reach into the most intimate corners of life? The answer has often been a balance between fear and obedience, with occasional sparks of resistance from dissident movements, journalists, and civil society organizations. The next section considers a different approach to addressing past crimes—how societies try to reckon with what has come before when new governments rise from the ashes: transitional justice.

TRANSITIONAL JUSTICE: TRUTH COMMISSIONS, AMNESTY, AND RETRIBUTION

When a regime falls or a society turns a corner after decades of repression, the moment demands more than new laws; it demands a way to narrate the past that can sustain a future. Transitional justice is the suite of strategies societies adopt to respond to crimes once they have lost their immediate political utility as instruments of control. It seeks a balance between accountability and peace, memory and reconciliation, punishment and healing. The tools are varied, and their coherence is often contested. Truth commissions, amnesty laws, retributive prosecutions, vetting processes for public officials, and reparations programs all claim a stake in this shared project of coming to terms with history.

South Africa's Truth and Reconciliation Commission stands as a landmark example. Its architecture was novel: public hearings that allowed victims to tell their stories, amnesty for perpetrators who disclosed full truths, and the delicate calculus of restoring dignity while acknowledging deep wounds. The aim was not to erase the past but to render it legible in a way that could prevent its recurrence. Amnesties offered a bitter compromise: some truth can only arrive at the price of impunity for others, while many survivors embraced the possibility of official acknowledgment even as it did not erase their pain.

In Latin America and elsewhere, transitional justice took other paths. Argentina's juntas, Chile's dictatorship, Peru's violence, and several nations in Central America and East Asia experimented with commissions, trials, pardons, and reparations. The debates were inevitably thorny. Does justice require punishment for every atrocity, or can truth and reparations offer a better path to national healing? How do you reconcile the needs of victims with the political realities of a fragile democracy that must move forward? And who bears responsibility when leaders who ordered crimes are protected by complex webs of power and influence that outlast the regime itself?

Transitional justice is not a guarantee of moral repair, nor is it a final accounting. It is an ongoing process, often a negotiation among memory, power, and aspiration. It asks societies to decide whether they want to prevent the past from becoming the present in future forms of governance. It invites reflection on what justice looks like when normal legal channels have been undermined by war, repression, or collapse. And it reminds us that punishment, however necessary, remains only one instrument among many in the long work of building a more just world.

NINE
RIGHTS, REFORMS, AND REVOLTS: THE LATE-20TH-CENTURY CRIMINAL JUSTICE TURN

NEW CODES, NEW NATIONS

When the banners of independence rose across the globe, former colonies faced a stubborn truth: laws move with power, and power is now theirs to define. The moment of decolonization was not only about who governed, but how justice would be imagined in a newly sovereign state. In many places the old colonial penal codes remained the skeleton of the system but were suddenly paired with the heartbeat of a nation in the making. Parties to independence demanded legitimacy and sovereignty, and that meant rewriting the scripts that governed crime, punishment, and policing. Yet the act of rewriting proved messier than a simple replacement. Legal independence did not wipe away the structures of control that had been built up over decades. Police forces, court procedures, and correctional institutions often carried with them the memory of state power as it was exercised under empire. The result was a paradox: a fresh constitution on paper, a continuity of enforcement on the street.

In practice, new governments faced a daunting task: craft criminal codes that reflected local values while maintaining order and legitimacy in a world where foreign powers and international norms still weighed on every decision. Some nations moved quickly to lay out modern rights—inclusion of due process, protections against arbitrary detention, and clearer standards for evidence. Others adopted hybrid systems, keeping familiar colonial instruments but rebranding them with local names. The reform was rarely linear. In some places, codes that criminalized political dissent remained in place long after independence, becoming tools of factional governance. In others, reformers pushed ahead with radical reshaping of police powers, juvenile justice, and standards for trials, all in the name of national dignity and social progress.

Decolonization did not occur in a vacuum. World War II and its aftermath pushed a universal conversation about rights, sovereignty, and the legitimacy of state coercion. The same era that produced universal declarations also produced the hard realities of local politics: ethnic tensions, land reform, economic struggles, and the fear that newly powerful actors might treat crime as a convenient lever to consolidate control. As a result, the criminal code in a newly independent state often became a battleground for identity and legitimacy as much as for crime and punishment.

In many places, the legacy of colonial policing persisted in the form of investigative techniques, arrest powers, surveillance practices, and the routine targeting of marginalized communities. Reformers argued that a freshly minted state needed a policing framework that could survive scrutiny, endure corruption, and stand up to political pressure. They sought professionalization—training for officers, clearer lines of accountability, and a justice system that protected basic rights without becoming a playground for corruption or fear. Yet the effort to balance security with liberty was rarely clean. Some regimes used the reform impulse to pursue social control with greater sophistication, crafting modern-sounding codes that still served authoritarian ends. Others built institutions from scratch in a bid to reflect local philosophies of justice—indigenous restorative practices, community policing models, and legal philosophies that foregrounds communal welfare over punitive zeal.

What emerged, then, was a mosaic: no single revolution of the law across the globe, but many revolutions, each shaped by local history, international pressures, and the stubborn human desire to feel safe. De jure independence and de facto security often traveled on separate rails. The old codes granted the new states a vocabulary for punishment, but the manner in which those words were enforced—how protectively rights were read, how quickly suspects were processed, how transparent trials could be—became the test of sovereignty itself. This section invites you to see that moment not as a neat transition but as a tense negotiation between the old guard's tools and the new nation's hopes. It is a reminder that the history of crime and punishment always begins with the questions sovereignty raises: Who gets to decide what counts as crime? Whose lives are valued in the enforcement of the law? And how can a state prove that its pursuit of order is compatible with the dignity of its people?

RIGHTS IN THE STREET

The street became a stage where the promises of independence confronted the stubborn habits of policing. Across continents, people took to plazas, ports, and capital avenues to demand that the new states honor the rights they had asserted in constitutions and charters. The stage was not only political; it was deeply personal. When crowds gathered to demand fair treatment, to protest wrongful arrests, to insist that the law protect rather than punish their communities, the state learned quickly that legitimacy slipped through its fingers whenever policing felt arbitrary, cruel, or biased.

In practice, decolonizing nations confronted the same central dilemma: how to secure order without turning the clock back on rights. The answer varied. Some adopted robust due-process protections as a public commitment, writing into law safeguards against unlawful detention, guarantees of legal counsel, and clearer definitions of how evidence could be used. Others moved more cautiously, prioritizing political stability and economic reconstruction, which sometimes meant tight controls on assembly, speech, and association. The result was a spectrum from court-centered reform to executive-style intervention where the police acted as guardians of national unity rather than a neutral force for justice.

Civil rights movements at home and anti-colonial campaigns abroad fed into these debates. The modern idea of policing by consent—police answering to the communities they serve—was tested in cities long accustomed to hierarchical, punitive policing structures. It was not simply a matter of creating new rules; it was a reeducation of what police were for and who they were protecting. Activists argued that the legitimacy of law depended on visible accountability and the right to a fair hearing. Governments, watching the momentum of international opinion and the fear of social disorder, sometimes embraced reforms gradually. Others resisted changes, arguing that the harshness of the past was a necessary shield against chaos. The tension between reform and control defined this era, as new nations learned to defend themselves with laws that could, if properly implemented, feel both just and practical.

The local and the global overlapped in surprising ways. International donors, treaty obligations, and regional courts began pressing for standards that could be measured and defended. The new codes were meant to serve as a badge of sovereignty, yet they had to operate within a world where crime did not respect borders. Decolonization therefore produced more than a legal makeover; it produced a culture of rights that would take decades to fully take root in everyday policing. It also reminded readers that the law is never simply a set of rules; it is a living instrument that must earn the trust of the people it governs. A nation's right to govern is, in large part, the right to be fair in the eyes of its own citizens.

HEALTH, FEAR, AND PUNISHMENT: THE WAR ON DRUGS

The late decades of the twentieth century rewrote the language of crime as much as the landscape of punishment. In many places the narrative of drug use shifted from a health crisis to a public safety crisis, and then to a political battleground. The shift did not happen by accident. It followed economic anxieties, the fear of urban disintegration, and a media narrative that framed drug use as a moral failure linked to violence, decay, and social decay. When politics took control of the policy needle, consequences followed not only in the balance sheets of governments but in the lives of millions who found themselves swept up in a punitive system that seemed to multiply the problems it claimed to solve.

The transformation was dramatic. Policies that had once favored treatment and rehabilitation became weapons of deterrence and punishment. The social contract that had promised assistance for addiction, mental health supports, and public health interventions gave way to sentencing disciplines that sought to deter through severity. Mandatory minimums tightened the screws, stripping judges of discretion and turning the outcome of a single offense into a fixed, compulsory sentence. The rhetoric of crime and punishment found a home in campaign slogans, in political ads, and in the fear that without tough measures, cities would unravel.

In parallel, some voices argued for a humanitarian reversal. Public health perspectives that framed drug use as a medical issue began to gain traction in certain jurisdictions. Treatment programs, harm-reduction strategies, and decriminalization experiments offered a counterpoint to the punitive drumbeat. The contrast was not merely philosophical; it was practical. The same streets that had seen crackdowns and mass arrests also bore witness to reform efforts aimed at reducing harm, addressing the root causes of addiction, and redirecting resources toward prevention and recovery. The war on drugs thus became a lived laboratory of policy trade-offs: how to balance fear with evidence, punishment with opportunity, and the public's sense of safety with the basic dignity owed to every person.

Across continents, countries grappled with their own versions of the same dilemma: to protect society from the harms of drug use without erasing the humanity of those affected. The policy choices of this era created winners and losers in clear, painful terms. They also seeded a political culture in which drugs, crime, and punishment would forever be entwined, a reminder that the state's approach to addiction tells us much about its approach to the vulnerable and the voiceless.

RISING VOICES, SHIFTING FATES: VICTIMS, VOICES, AND TOUGH ON CRIME

The postwar era saw an ascent of victims' voices into the public sphere. No longer satisfied with being silent witnesses to the consequences of crime, many people who had suffered—families of murder victims, survivors of assault, communities wrecked by violence—began to demand a seat at the policy table. The turn toward acknowledging victims' rights did not arrive as a perfectly uniform movement. It arrived as a chorus, with different notes in different places, but with a shared insistence that the system owed them a place at every stage of criminal justice—from investigation to sentencing to parole.

This demand reshaped the rhetoric of punishment. Policies began to respond to victims' experiences: the right to be heard at sentencing, the opportunity to provide impact statements, and a louder, more visible voice in parole decisions. At times the result was a hardening effect, as campaigns invoked victims' stories to justify longer sentences and fewer opportunities for release. The political calculus of fear often trumped the pragmatic desire to reduce harm through rehabilitation. Yet the era also produced openings for reform. Victims' groups urged transparency, accountability, and reformist ideas that could balance the scales between public safety and mercy. Restorative justice, family impact statements, and victim-offender mediation found space in a landscape that had previously offered little more than a specter of retribution.

The paradox at the heart of this shift is revealing. The same voices that pressed for greater visibility and protection for victims also catalyzed a broader conversation about how to reduce crime and suffering in the long run. In some places, a new tonal shift toward accountability brought about smarter policies: targeted interventions for high-risk offenders, community oversight of policing, and a demand that the system repair harm rather than simply punish it. In others, the rhetoric of victims' rights became a banner under which punitive policies flourished, even when the outcomes harmed the very communities those policies claimed to serve. The chapter's through line is clear: reform movements rarely arrive as a single, neat reform. They come as a chorus of competing aims, each promising justice, each carrying a different price.

The late twentieth century thus gave birth to a complex, at times contradictory, set of reforms. Victims' voices made the debate more humane in some respects, more punitive in others. The moral calculus of punishment shifted, not because one side won permanently, but because society learned to listen to new kinds of suffering while still wrestling with the fear that crime, if left unchecked, would devour the fabric of community life.

THE ERA OF FEAR: THREE STRIKES AND THE MINIMUMS

The political climate of the late twentieth century gave rise to a relentless drumbeat: crime is rising, punishment must rise faster. A chorus of political leaders promised safety by signing on to hard, unmistakable rules. The idea was simple in its rhetoric: punish more, punish longer, intervene earlier, and keep repeat offenders off the street. The mechanism was equally simple: mandatory minimum sentences and three-strikes laws that removed the discretion of judges and turned a single conviction into a life sentence for some offenders. The appeal to public fear was powerful. Campaigns framed crime as an existential threat to families, neighborhoods, and social order. The language of crisis, while emotionally persuasive, hid complex truths about crime rates, policing practices, and the social conditions that produce criminal behavior.

In practice, the effects were uneven but real. Judges found themselves bound by fixed sentences that sometimes produced disproportionate penalties for relatively minor offenses. The public saw a dramatic increase in the number of people kept in prison for extended periods, and communities that had long borne the brunt of policing discovered that the new statutes often intensified the very harms they sought to prevent. Racial disparities appeared with painful clarity as marginalized communities became the primary recipients of punitive policy.

Three strikes and mandatory minimums did not simply expand punishment. They also reshaped the incentives within the legal system. Prosecutors gained leverage in plea bargaining as a means to secure meaningful sentences quickly. Defense lawyers found themselves navigating increasingly rigid rules that limited their ability to argue for individualized circumstances. In the public arena, however, the message of deterrence resonated across party lines, and the campaigns that championed tough-on-crime policies enjoyed broad support. The legacy of this era is contested: it is a record of attempts to respond to fear with certainty, and a reminder that certainty in punishment comes at the cost of nuance, mercy, and the possibility of second chances.

THE PRISON BOOM: MASS INCARCERATION AND ITS CONSEQUENCES

The late twentieth century did not merely reframe punishment; it exploded its reach. Prison populations swelled beyond anything seen in previous eras. The new carceral state stretched across cities and rural counties, in nations and regions, as the number of people behind bars climbed into the millions. The social landscape shifted around this towering statistic. Families were fractured, communities destabilized, and generations of young people found themselves shaped by the daily reality of surveillance, stigma, and confinement. The consequences extended beyond the individuals incarcerated to the communities that bore the burden of the system's costs and its failures to address underlying causes like poverty, education gaps, and mental health needs.

Economically, the burden was enormous. Tax dollars flowed to build, staff, and maintain facilities, while money that could have funded schools, housing, and healthcare was redirected toward cages and corrections software. The social costs were equally steep. Children of incarcerated parents faced higher risk of poverty, academic difficulties, and future involvement with crime. Racial disparities in sentencing and incarceration became one of the era's most troubling legacies, reminding readers that punishment, even when framed as a universal remedy, often operates through a racialized logic that multiplies harm for already marginalized groups.

The private sector sometimes found profit in the policy design. Prisons and probation services became commodities, raising questions about profit incentives in a system that should be about public safety and rehabilitation. Critics argued that this created perverse incentives to keep people in cages longer and to rely on punishment as a primary tool rather than an instrument of hope. Supporters, meanwhile, claimed that efficiency and innovation came with privatization and competition. The truth lay somewhere in between: institutions modernized, but the moral economy of punishment grew more complex and contested.

Mass incarceration, with all its social costs, did not come without countercurrents. Reform advocates pointed to the data that showed the limitations of confinement as a tool for reducing crime. They asked how communities might rebuild in the wake of mass imprisonment. They pointed to alternatives—restorative justice approaches, community-led policing reforms, educational and employment opportunities for those reentering society, and sentencing reforms that recognized rehabilitation as a possibility as well as a right. The story of the late twentieth century's turn is thus not only about the scale of punishment but about the realization that the cost of punishment, if not paired with opportunity, can undermine the very safety that punishment purports to protect.

TEN
CYBERCRIME, SURVEILLANCE, AND THE ALGORITHMIC FUTURE OF PUNISHMENT

HACKERS, FRAUDSTERS, AND DARK WEB MARKETS: NEW FRONTIERS OF CRIME

Across the twenty-first century, crime has not vanished; it has migrated into cyberspace. The old tools are still dangerous, but now the weapon is code. Hackers, organized crime groups, fraudsters, and vigilante data pirates move through digital corridors where speed, anonymity, and global reach outrun borders. The most chilling thing about cybercrime is not necessarily the violence but the scale and the invisibility. A single phishing email can start a chain reaction that bankrupts a hospital, a small business, or a city's water utility.

In this chapter we explore major forms: hacking, ransomware, business email compromise, identity theft, and a spectrum of online fraud that mimics traditional scams but travels at the speed of servers and satellites. Then we meet the dark web, a marketplace that makes illegal goods and services accessible to anyone with crypto and a browser. Marketplaces flourish where trust is scarce and verification is spotty. The phrase crime as a service captures the sense that criminal capabilities are increasingly commodified—tools, infrastructure, and expertise sold to the highest bidder. Ransomware kits that can be rented, botnets that can be leased, even covert services like doxxing and social-engineering campaigns—these do not require a seasoned gang with a long history of violence. A competent attacker can assemble a credible operation from components available online.

This shift changes the calculus of risk for offenders and defenders alike. The territory of crime has shifted from smoky backrooms and border crossings to cloud servers and encrypted chats. Victims range from individuals whose identities are harvested to institutions that must reboot entire networks after a breach. Hospitals once left their doors open to the world; now they fear not only pathogen outbreaks but the digital kind—the ransomware that locks their life-support systems and extorts payment. Utilities, schools, financial services, and small merchants all sit on the same internet-backed fault line. The cost of a cyberattack is no longer confined to a single moment in time; it ripples through supply chains, emergency responses, and public trust.

Law enforcement and policy makers are forced to chase a moving target. Cybercrime units, specialized prosecutors, and international task forces race to keep up with evolving tools. Cooperation across borders becomes not a courtesy but a necessity, because a criminal operation that lives in one country can exploit networks, servers, and payment rails in many others. Yet the speed and reach of digital crime create profound governance challenges: how to attribute responsibility, how to seize illicit assets that cross jurisdictions in seconds, and how to balance security with civil liberties. Encryption expands the safety margin for everyday privacy while simultaneously shielding criminals from ordinary forms of detection. Transparency and accountability must keep pace with innovation, or the same technologies that empower citizens will also empower malefactors.

The horizon holds a paradox: as technology escalates the scale and sophistication of crime, it also equips defenders with new weapons. Threat intelligence feeds, network forensics, and machine-learning-driven anomaly detection are increasingly effective at stopping intrusions before they bloom into costly incidents. But we must acknowledge human factors—phishing remains the easiest path for many criminals, and social engineering thrives on misused trust. In the end, the history of punishment in the digital age will hinge on how societies integrate technical resilience with robust rights protections, how quickly responders learn from each breach, and how vigilantly we cultivate a culture of security without surrendering the freedoms that give technology its promise.

POLICING BY NUMBERS: PREDICTIVE ANALYTICS AND RISK SCORES

If crime is now a function of data, then policing cannot escape data's logic. Predictive analytics, risk scoring, and algorithmic triage promise to allocate attention, resources, and responses with unprecedented precision. The idea is seductive: look to the past, map the patterns, and anticipate the future. In practice, this means maps of crime hotspots, dashboards that flag potential threats, and tools that help decide where to send patrols or how to allocate detectives. It also means that decisions about liberty—urging a suspect to comply with bail conditions, or prioritizing a witness for protection—are increasingly mediated by numbers.

One of the most familiar applications is the use of risk assessments at various points of the criminal process. Judges, prosecutors, and probation officers rely on scores that purport to estimate a defendant's likelihood of reoffending, or a pretrial defendant's risk of flight. These tools synthesize a flood of variables: prior arrest histories, demographics, residence stability, employment, and sometimes even more sensitive data such as neighborhood crime rates. The algebra of these scores is not simple; it is a translation of complex, real-world life into probabilities. In the best scenarios, predictive analytics can target interventions where they matter most, reduce wasteful policing, and prevent harm before it arises.

But numbers are not neutral. Algorithms inherit the biases of the data on which they are trained, and those biases can amplify disparities in the criminal-legal system. If past policing practices have over-policed certain communities, predictive models may reinforce that over-policing by directing more attention to precisely those neighborhoods. If pretrial risk assessments weigh on factors correlated with race, class, or geographic location, they risk entrenching unfair outcomes behind a veneer of objectivity. The central questions are not technical alone but political and ethical: who gets to see the models, what inputs are considered legitimate, and how transparent should the process be when life-changing decisions hinge on an algorithm's recommendation? Accountability becomes both a design problem and a governance problem.

Advocates emphasize the gains: smoother case flow, faster triage, the possibility of keeping communities safer by focusing resources more efficiently. Critics warn of overreach and surveillance creep, of chilling effects that push vulnerable people away from essential supports. The challenge is to harness the strengths of data science while building guardrails that protect due process, privacy, and human judgment. The future of crime prevention will likely rest on a calibration between predictive power and human oversight—an honest conversation about where data helps and where it harms, and how to design systems that serve justice rather than merely speed it along.

CAMERAS EVERYWHERE: CCTV, BODYCAMS, AND FACIAL RECOGNITION

In cities around the world, cameras have become the architectural punctuation of public life. From subway tunnels to school corridors, from high streets to hospital hallways, the gaze of the state—and increasingly that of private platforms and corporations—tracks, records, and sometimes judges each moment. The promise is simple: deterrence, rapid response, and a corpus of evidence that makes prosecution more straightforward. The reality is more complicated. Surveillance can deter crime, or it can chill lawful activity. It can enable swift interventions, but it can also chill the voices of dissent and ordinary civic life.

CCTV networks have matured into expansive, data-rich ecosystems. Some cities boast hundreds of thousands of cameras watching streets, transit centers, and critical infrastructure. The results are appealing in the abstract: better traffic management, quicker identification of suspects, faster incident response. But the accountability scaffolding—who surveils the surveillers, how long footage is stored, who can access it, and for what purposes —remains underdeveloped in many jurisdictions. The temptation to extend the net—to save a few hours of investigative labor—collides with larger concerns about privacy, consent, and civil liberties.

Then there is the new generation of visual technologies: body-worn cameras for police, and facial recognition algorithms that promise to identify individuals in real time. Bodycams have become a symbol of accountability, yet their impact is uneven. Some departments report improved behavior and fewer complaints; others face questions about when and how video is released, or whether footage is weaponized to shape public narratives. Facial recognition, meanwhile, provokes the fiercest debates. When the technology misidentifies people, especially those from marginalized communities, trust in the whole system erodes. The reliability disparities—accuracy is often higher for well-lit, high-contrast images, and lower for darker skin tones or complex angles—underscore a core tension: tools designed to make the state more precise can, paradoxically, make the system less fair if not carefully governed.

Oversight bodies, independent audits, and clear data-minimization policies are not luxuries but necessities. Without them, the very benefits of surveillance risk becoming the fuel for abuse. Public trust depends on transparent purposes, robust safeguards, and visible consequences when the system goes wrong. The balance is delicate: security and privacy must coevolve, not collide, as the digital eye becomes a ubiquitous feature of modern life.

BORDERS, TERRORISM, AND GLOBAL POLICING NETWORKS

The twenty-first century has reimagined the border as a network rather than a line. Data flows leap across oceans long before people do, and the tools of security—biometrics, travel histories, and interoperable databases—span continents as easily as a passport once crossed a desk. Counterterrorism, migration control, and transnational crime all rely on a shared, sometimes contested, constellation of information-sharing agreements. The speed and reach of these networks have produced undeniable security gains: faster watchlists, better risk assessments at immigration checkpoints, and more effective interdiction of illicit funds and contraband. They have also raised serious questions about sovereignty, consent, and civil liberties in a world where data can travel as freely as people.

At the heart of this system are the networks that knit together police, intelligence agencies, and private sector partners. Interoperability is celebrated as cost-saving and life-saving, but it also creates systemic vulnerabilities. One breach in a centralized database can expose millions of records, sparking fears about identity theft, stigmatization, and the misuse of biometric data. Legal frameworks struggle to keep pace with rapid tech-enabled practices: data retention periods that seem reasonable in one country can feel invasive or unnecessary in another, and the rules about who has access to data can vary as widely as the languages spoken in those countries.

Migration has become a flashpoint for these global policing networks. The same systems that allow authorities to identify potential threats can also flag innocent travelers, enforce harsh border policies, or criminalize asylum seekers through automated indicators. Critics warn that data-driven borders may treat people as algorithms instead of as human beings, prioritizing risk containment over humane outcomes. Proponents argue that targeted controls prevent harm and reduce the need for more coercive measures later. The tension between security and rights is not a mere footnote; it is the defining scale on which the twenty-first century is measured.

The real test, then, is not whether states can collect more data but whether they can govern it wisely. Transparent governance, independent oversight, and meaningful pathways for redress become as essential as the tools themselves. The future of border security will hinge on a social contract that accepts risk while protecting dignity, a balance that will require constant calibration as technology evolves.

CORPORATE CRIME AND FINANCIAL SCANDALS: WHEN THE POWERFUL BREAK THE RULES

If the digital era has democratized access to information, it has also intensified the temptations for those who control capital and markets. Corporate crime in the twenty-first century sits at the intersection of technology, finance, and governance. White-collar offenses—fraud, market manipulation, bribery, and insider dealing—continue to test the limits of criminal law. They are not always dramatic in the courtroom; often they unfold in spreadsheets, regulatory filings, and the quiet compliance meetings where the line between clever risk-taking and illegal behavior blurs. When powerful actors bend the rules, victims include employees, investors, employees' families, and sometimes entire economies.

The digital age adds new textures to old crimes. Data manipulation, misrepresentation of financial health through dashboards and code, and the deliberate misdirection of audits can be as damaging as a classic heist. The availability of digital tools also lowers the barriers to wrongdoing: sophisticated scams that would have required a gang's coordination are now plausible for individuals acting alone or in small teams. And the digital economy has created new assets—cryptocurrencies, tokenized securities, offshore digital wallets—that complicate enforcement, laundering, and tracing of illicit gains.

The question of punishment for corporate crime remains contested. Fines, often measured in hundreds of millions or billions of dollars, are common, but critics argue that penalties are insufficient deterrents when profits from wrongdoing still exceed the cost of getting caught. Prosecutors increasingly deploy instruments such as deferred prosecution agreements and corporate compliance monitors to induce reform, but these measures can feel like a cost of doing business rather than a genuine impediment. Independent investigations and robust whistleblower protections play a crucial role in revealing malfeasance that crowded boardrooms would prefer to overlook.

Ethics and accountability have to extend beyond the balance sheet. Public confidence depends on the belief that the powerful will be held to the same standards as everyone else, and that law enforcement will pursue wrongdoing regardless of profit or reputation. The modern story of corporate crime is not merely about clever loopholes or clever lawyers; it is about whether institutions can withstand temptations posed by scale, speed, and the temptations of anonymity in a digital world.

DIGITAL TRAILS AND SOCIAL CREDIT: PUNISHMENT BEYOND THE PRISON

The penumbra of punishment now stretches far beyond the prism of jail doors. Every online action, every data point, leaves a digital trace that can shape futures in subtle and sometimes brutal ways. Deplatforming, demonetization, and selective throttling of access to services are the most visible forms of reputational punishment in the digital era. A person's online presence becomes a kind of credit history in a marketplace where trust is monetized. Employers, landlords, insurers, and even healthcare providers frequently consult digital footprints to assess risk, suitability, or reliability. A misstep online can reverberate for years, just as a violent act might haunt a person's past. The threshold between personal history and public judgment grows thinner with each social post, review, and click.

Beyond platform-based penalties, broader systems resemble a modern version of social credit. In some places, state-run or platform-driven scoring aggregates a citizen's or consumer's behavior into a numerical profile that influences access to credit, housing, or travel. The risk is not only exclusion but the invisibility of the mechanism: people can be penalized without a court hearing or a transparent rationale. In other contexts, the law itself uses digital trails to extend consequences—pretrial conditions enforced by remote monitoring, or post-release supervision wherein digital location data become a condition of freedom.

This is not merely an extension of punishment; it is a redefinition of punishment. The public sphere, market access, and even daily services can hinge on a person's standing in data ecosystems. Critics call for principled limits: data minimization, narrow purposes, transparent algorithms, and explicit rights to contest or delete records. Proponents argue that reputational penalties reflect accountability—breaches of trust in a data-driven economy deserve consequences. The question, once again, is balance. How do societies protect the public from harm while guarding against the creation of a permanent, opaque blacklist that follows people through every phase of life? The path forward will require constant vigilance, deliberate governance, and a willingness to place human judgment above machine outputs when lives and livelihoods hang in the balance.

IMAGINING JUSTICE DIFFERENTLY: A CONCLUSION ON CRIME, PUNISHMENT, AND POSSIBILITY

WHAT HISTORY TEACHES

History does not march in a straight line. It moves in fits and starts, propelled by fear, hunger for power, moments of illumination, and stubborn stubbornness. When we read the long arc of crime and punishment, patterns appear as clearly as fingerprints on a glass: cycles of threat and response, shifts in who counts as a threat, and a recurrent refrain—that punishment is supposed to make us safer, just, and free. Yet the pages also show that safety is not a single outcome, and justice never lands in a single way. It arrives wrapped in culture, technology, and the politics of who is eligible for mercy.

Across civilizations and centuries, fear often drives punishment more than abstract ideals of right. In ancient courts, threats to a community's survival justified violent penalties. In early modern states, spectacles of punishment were as much about teaching obedience as they were about justice. Over and over, reformers arrive with the conviction that cruelty is a mistake, only to discover that reform morsels are easily eaten by political appetites hungry for control. These patterns are not random; they are shaped by who holds the levers of power, who is made to bear the cost of crime, and what technologies and ideas help a society label a wrong as an offense rather than a disease, a sin, or a rebellion.

What surprises us most, perhaps, is the stubborn persistence of harm even as systems multiply rules and institutions. The spread of trial by jury, the rise of forensic science, the professionalization of policing, and the expansion of prisons have all given the illusion that we have finally tamed crime. Yet the same epochs reveal the reappearance of new forms of harm—systems that fail to address root causes, overpolicing in marginalized neighborhoods, and the criminalization of poverty and dissent. The myths we tell about progress—that punishment grows more precise, more humane, more protective of rights with every leap forward—are seductive. They are not wrong, but they are incomplete.

So what does history actually teach us? That justice is a living project, braided with power, scarcity, and culture; that fear can be used to justify extraordinary measures; and that reform cycles are real—sometimes lifting communities, sometimes plateauing into new methods of control. The past shows that change is possible, but it is not guaranteed. It shows, too, that the shape of punishment often reflects the prevailing story about who counts as a person and what counts as harm. If we want to reimagine the future, we must listen to these stories with an eye for what they reveal about values as much as about numbers. The history invites us to ask not only how to punish differently, but how to live together with more care, more accountability, and more imagination.

In this light, the chapters that came before can be read as a long experiment in collective judgment. The rise and fall of cruel spectacles, the slow birth of rights, the entry of science into the courtroom, and the stubborn endurance of inequality all contribute to a single point: the past is testimony, not destiny. Understanding the patterns, myths, and surprises of history means learning to separate the useful lessons from the seductive simplifications. It means recognizing that our ideas about crime and punishment are not fixed answers but choices we make together, over and over again. And it means honoring the stories of those who bore the burden of punishment and those who carried the weight of resistance, so that future choices might be wiser, fairer, and more humane.

THE LIMITS OF PUNISHMENT: WHAT PRISONS AND POLICING CANNOT DO

If we look honestly at the record, punishment solves few of crime's deepest problems. Deterrence—the idea that fear of punishment will stop people from offending—looks smaller when we compare different eras and different places. Some societies with harsh penalties have long experienced persistent cycles of crime and harm, while others with more measured, targeted responses have seen safer streets and more stable communities. The bigger truth is that fear alone does not address what creates crime in the first place: inequality, lack of opportunity, trauma, and the conditions that shape choices under pressure. Prisons cannot fully separate offenders from the social worlds that produced them, and they cannot repair the broken ties that make reoffending seem rational to someone in pain.

Prisons serve as containment more than cure. They remove a person from a particular social setting, yes, but they rarely remove the risk they carry into the future. Recidivism remains stubbornly high in many systems, not because individuals lack will or capacity for change, but because the surrounding ecosystems—housing, jobs, family support, mental health care—have not kept pace with the need for transformation. When the focus is punishment rather than safety, the cost is often borne by families and communities who bear the consequences of separation, stigma, and economic deprivation. And policing—when framed as a single instrument of enforcement—inevitably becomes a story about control rather than safety. The most revealing findings show that aggressive policing, mass surveillance, and zero-tolerance policies rarely predict safer streets; they predict more contact with the system, more mistrust, and more harm to those who already stand on the margins.

The limits are not only moral; they are empirical. Forensic breakthroughs can convict with increasing certainty, and yet conviction does not guarantee a safer citizenry. Rehabilitation programs, when they exist, require sustained investment, individualized attention, and social supports that continue after release. Time and again, the evidence suggests that punishment without healing—without addressing the roots of harm, without offering meaningful paths to reintegration—produces harm that echoes through generations. If we measure safety by the absence of harm and the presence of opportunity, we must admit that punishment alone cannot deliver either. The limits of punishment invite a braver question: what if safety and care could be pursued in ways that do not depend on confinement, surveillance, or spectacle?

This is not a naive critique of institutions. It is a call to understand that punishment is at best partial, at worst harmful when used as a default solution. It asks us to consider whether there are other levers—investments in education, housing, healthcare, and community safety—

that can reduce harm more reliably and humanely than prisons ever have. The chapter that follows will explore those levers, not as fantasies but as practical, tested, and sometimes radical alternatives that reframe crime as social harm rather than personal punishment. The goal is not to abolish accountability but to reimagine accountability in ways that center repair, safety, and dignity for everyone involved.

RESTORATIVE AND TRANSFORMATIVE JUSTICE: REPAIRING HARM WITHOUT REVENGE

Restorative justice begins with a simple, uncomfortable premise: most wrongs harm relationships before they harm individuals. If crime is a rupture in a web of people and communities, healing must start with those who bear the cost of that rupture—the victims, the community, and the offender who takes responsibility. The approach shifts the center of gravity from punishment to repair. It invites meaningfully engaging those most affected by crime in decisions about how to respond, rebuild trust, and prevent further harm.

The practice takes many forms, from mediated conversations and circles to community conferences and reparative agreements. In some settings, victims and offenders sit in the same room; in others, they do not. What matters is the core idea: accountability is not a sentence; it is a process of acknowledging harm, understanding its roots, and choosing concrete steps to repair what was broken. This often includes restitution, but restitution is only one tool among many. A restorative frame can also demand changes in a community's social structure, access to services, and commitments to ongoing safety.

Restorative justice works best when it is voluntary, adequately resourced, and guided by trained facilitators who understand power dynamics and trauma. It requires careful attention to safety—ensuring that victims feel heard, respected, and protected—and it demands clarity about what counts as completion of the process. In many places, restorative programs have grown from pilot projects into mainstream options within schools, youth courts, and neighborhoods. They have also faced serious challenges: concerns about equity, potential coercion, and the problem of how to scale a fundamentally relational practice.

The most compelling pilots show what is possible when communities choose care as their default. In those spaces, healing moves beyond a single incident toward a broader commitment to preventing harm. Victims report feeling seen; offenders report a chance to repair what they broke; communities gain a stake in turning away from cycles of retaliation. The transformation is not magical; it is painstaking, relational work. It requires time, patience, and generous resources. Yet the payoff can be profound: safer neighborhoods built on trust, not fear, and a justice that respects the humanity of all involved.

ABOLITIONIST THOUGHT: RETHINKING SAFETY WITHOUT MASS INCARCERATION

Abolitionist thought does not begin with a denial of harm. It begins with a radical claim: that a system centered on punishment is not the only—or even the best—way to keep people safe. Visionaries in this tradition argue that safety is inseparable from social provision. If a society cannot ensure housing, health, education, and economic opportunity for all of its members, it will continue to rely on prisons as a default solution to a problem that is not primarily a criminal problem but a social one.

Abolitionists pursue decarceration and reform as practical strategy rather than as abstract principle. They advocate for eliminating cash bail, reducing the reach of the criminal law, and diverting funds from incarceration toward prevention, mental health care, housing, and jobs programs. They argue for replacing some offenses with public health responses, not to excuse harm but to address its underlying causes. Portugal's drug policies, for example, show how decriminalization—paired with robust health and social services—can reduce harm and reclaim a sense of public safety that does not rely on punishment as the primary tool.

The abolitionist project also involves reimagining accountability. If prisons disappear or shrink dramatically, who answers for wrongdoing? The answer is not chaos but communities organizing around care, safety planning, and proportional responses that avoid the moral bifurcation of "innocent vs. guilty." This is not cynicism about justice; it is a hopeful assertion that a world with fewer punitive walls might be more just, more humane, and more resilient. Yet abolitionists are clear about the scale of the challenge: it requires retooling institutions, rethinking budgets, and rebuilding social fabrics that have frayed under decades of punitive policy. It invites a long game, one in which reforms are measured not by the number of people released but by the number of harms prevented and the number of lives restored to communities.

Ultimately, abolitionist thought asks a provocative question: what if safety could be produced by care rather than coercion? It dares to imagine a future in which the default response to harm is not punishment but repair, not suspicion but solidarity, not exclusion but inclusion. It is less a blueprint than a challenge to widen the circle of responsibility and to test new forms of accountability that center humanity and dignity for every person.

GLOBAL EXPERIMENTS: FROM DECRIMINALIZATION TO COMMUNITY POLICING

Around the world, pilots and programs are testing what justice could look like when the old reflexes of punishment are tempered by care, evidence, and citizen participation. The stories are diverse, sometimes messy, and occasionally imperfect, but they share a common impulse: to break free from a one-size-fits-all approach to crime and to build responses that fit local needs and values.

Portugal's landmark decriminalization of drug use, paired with robust health and social supports, is often cited as a turning point. The policy did not legalize drugs; it redirected the energy of punishment into prevention, treatment, and social integration. The result was not chaos but a measurable reorientation of resources toward harm reduction, with modest or even favorable outcomes for public health and safety. In other places, decriminalization has followed different paths; Spain's coordinated approach to drug policy, or Uruguay's early experiments with regulatory frameworks around certain substances, illustrate how policy design matters as much as intent.

Restorative and community-based approaches have also gained traction in schools, workplaces, and neighborhoods. In many countries, youth courts, family-group conferences, and community mediation programs offer alternatives to automatic detention and suspension. In some cities, police reform efforts emphasize problem-oriented policing, neighborhood policing, and trauma-informed practices that seek to reduce unnecessary enforcement while increasing trust. These shifts are not uniform; they encounter political resistance, resource constraints, and concerns about safety. Yet they persist because communities witness tangible benefits: fewer repeat injuries, more cooperative relations with authorities, and a sense that public life is something communities can shape, not something imposed from above.

The most ambitious experiments lie in truth-telling and reconciliation—processes that acknowledge harm, recognize victims' experiences, and address structural injustices that no single statute can erase. In post-conflict settings and in societies wrestling with legacies of oppression, commissions and courts have offered avenues for accountability without erasure. These efforts do not erase pain; they weave it into a political education about what a community owes to its members and how it can prevent recurrence through collective care. They remind us that the road to safer futures is often paved with difficult conversations, inclusive decision-making, and sustained investment in people's lives.

Global experiments teach a crucial lesson: there is no single correct formula for safety or justice. There are, however, shared principles—connection, transparency, accountability, and the prioritizing of health and dignity—that tend to produce better outcomes than punishment alone. They also remind us that reform is a continuous project, not a single policy fix. When communities test, iterate, and learn, they generate knowledge that can travel across borders and transform how we think about crime, responsibility, and care.

REIMAGINING CRIME, RESPONSIBILITY, AND CARE: A HUMAN CHOICE OPEN TO CHANGE AND CREATIVITY

If the chapters before have shown anything, it is that human societies do not passively accept a single destiny for crime and punishment. We possess the imaginative capacity to redefine what counts as harm, who is responsible, and how communities can respond with courage, imagination, and fairness. The closing meditation of this book invites readers to see law not as fate but as a field of human choice—a set of instruments we may reconfigure in light of our deepest values.

The first move is to reframe crime as a social harm rather than solely a personal failing. When harm is understood in that way, prevention—through stable housing, mental health support, education, and economic opportunity—becomes a central justice act. Accountability then becomes a process of repair rather than a site of punishment. It invites those who have caused harm to acknowledge the impact, make amends, and participate in measures that reduce risk for others. This reframing does not excuse wrongdoing; it seeks to prevent harm in the first place and to restore relationships where possible.

Second, safety becomes a shared project. Communities build safety through public health, through trusted police practices that emphasize de-escalation and proportionality, and through structures that allow voices from all walks of life to shape policy. This means investing in places that often go underfunded: schools, clinics, housing, transportation, and community organizations. When safety is built with neighbors rather than imposed on them, it becomes a living, evolving practice rather than a distant ideal or a punitive threat.

Third, care must be extended to those who enforce the system. Police, prosecutors, judges, and corrections officers operate within incentives shaped by policy, training, and culture. Transforming justice therefore requires changing these incentives: reducing discretionary power where it hurts the vulnerable, expanding training in de-escalation and trauma, and offering pathways into humane, effective careers that serve the public good instead of controlling it. Caring for the people who enforce the system is inseparable from caring for the people who are affected by it.

Finally, the imagination is our most precious resource. The histories in this book have demonstrated that extraordinary changes can emerge from ordinary courage—the decision of a mayor to fund a community court, a prosecutor to try a restorative path, a neighborhood group to demand safer streets through investment rather than punishment. The future will not be born in a single reform, but in a tapestry of experiments that test new relationships between people, power, and policy. The invitation is to keep asking: What kind of justice do we want? What kind of society can we responsibly build? And how can we begin, today, with small steps that accumulate into bigger possibilities?

If we listen carefully to the past, we hear a chorus suggesting that the most humane, the most effective, and the most hopeful answer is not the hardest hammer we can raise, but the careful, persistent work of repairing, learning, and designing a justice that belongs to everyone.

www.ingramcontent.com/pod-product-compliance
Lightning Source LLC
Chambersburg PA
CBHW051549020426
42333CB00016B/2171